Copyright

Permission for Educational Use

This book was written to be used. Educators, caregivers, and youth-serving professionals are welcome to share and use selected tools, exercises, and excerpts from this book in classrooms, workshops, and noncommercial settings, with attribution.

For commercial use, training programs, or large-scale distribution, please contact the publisher for permission.

Use of these materials does not grant permission to create derivative works, curricula, or training programs for sale.

This book and its materials are for educational purposes only and are not a substitute for professional mental health treatment.

Cover and other graphics by Bounce Back Generation, Inc.

Published by https://generationbounceback.com/

ISBN Print: 979-8-9943724-1-8

Cover design and illustrations by Generation Bounce Back, SPC, and Bounce Back Generation, Inc.

How To Bounce Back

Emotional Evolution and the Science of Feeling Good

Jennifer K.W. Dhillon

Generation Bounce Back Media

Contents

Dedication 1

Preface 3

Introduction 9

1. It's Not Your Fault 13
2. You Are the Hero of Your Life 29
3. Taming Your Nervous System 55
4. Changing Your Belief Loops 85
5. Is Quantum Manifestation Real? 111
6. Introducing the 6 Building Blocks for Resilience 139
7. The Protection Building Block 155
8. The Relationship Building Block 161
9. The Belonging Building Block 179
10. The Coping Skills Building Block 189
11. The Confidence Building Block 209
12. The Storytelling Building Block 225

13. Emotions and Feelings 241
Epilogue 247
14. RESOURCES 255
About the author 263
About Bounce Back Generation 264

For my son, Taye

Preface

A Vision for Our Evolution

All that you touch you change. All that you change changes you.— Octavia Butler

Picture yourself drifting weightless in a spaceship humming gently above the Earth. The year is 2126. Unsnap your seatbelt and float along with me as we look down.

Something has happened on our home planet. It's still blue, lush, and green. But something has shifted.

People don't wake up with a feeling of dread and anxiety. Children play together outside without scanning the horizon for danger. Conversations feel gentler because people realize it's easier to be kind than to be competitive.

Life isn't perfect, but Earth is a harmonious and safe place to live, much more than it was a century ago.

Against all predictions, we are not being run by algorithms, artificial intelligence, or robot overlords. We run *them.*

Imagine that our planet is at peace. Wars have faded into history as a misguided pattern of violence. Humans now strive to cultivate positive feelings of mutual respect and connection across the globe and in space.

In this future world, we have learned how to regulate our nervous systems. We've found ways to release feelings of shame, fear, and aggression more easily. We have become experts at crafting beliefs that make us feel authentically powerful. We've mastered the ability to manifest our goals and realize the dreams we have for ourselves and our families.

We've evolved.

Now zoom back to today.

I believe we are standing at the threshold of a new kind of evolution — one not led by biological changes, but by emotional ones. Our next step must incorporate ways to feel good, to feel like we can manage state of mind, and that we can adjust our relationships with each other. Doing so gives us the capacity to evolve to the future I've just described.

Why is this possible now?

Science, mostly. We are the first generation in human history to understand the mechanics of our own suffering. Today, science is mapping how our biology, brain wiring, genetics, childhood experiences, and environments shape the way we feel, react, connect, and cope. We now know that trauma leaves traces in the body, that stress patterns can be inherited, and that our nervous system can get stuck in survival mode. These are things that left us feeling out of control of our moods and experiences.

But we also know this: the brain *can* change. Neural pathways can be rewired. We can reshape how we emotionally respond to adversity — and do so in ways that help us grow in personal power.

Some past experiences, especially in childhood, can feel like we have been left permanently damaged. But today we have hope for healing and, more importantly, prevention against long-term harm from trauma. With this information, we can greatly improve the odds for this, and future generations', well-being.

For centuries, our systems have focused on treating dysfunction after it appears. We've seen how addiction, anxiety, violence, and burnout are tolerated as normal in some communities. We have seen dysfunction among our political, moral, religious and corporate leaders become the norm and even celebrated as "strength."

As a nonprofit leader teaching resilience skills, and an attorney, I've been part of programs, courts, and correctional systems that are filled with young people who never had a chance, and adults who will spend their lives never having lived up to their potential.

But we now have the opportunity to change those doom and gloom projections.

We have the tools to interrupt cycles of trauma before they become part of a person's identity. We can teach children how to manage their nervous systems. We can help adults understand how their past shaped them and how to avoid being trapped by emotions they don't understand or find overwhelming. We have tools that can begin to heal generations who had to learn to survive in bodies that never felt safe.

We will see that our destiny isn't to bow to the intelligence of AI or technology. We are meant to dominate this planet through our unique human ability to feel, to seek out answers to moral questions, to create what has not been created, and to care for each other. Technology may out-think us, but it will never out-feel us. It is emotions that rule this world, not algorithms. This is the true value of humanity that we have yet to grasp and exploit.

Many people today (especially our young people) do not feel safe, yet they are labeled and punished for reactions, behaviors, and defenses that make sense in the context of our evolutionary development. We are a planet of people who are acting in ways *we have evolved to react* when we live in physically and emotionally difficult environments.

We can evolve our emotional responses so that we feel more powerful in the face of fear. We can prevent trauma, build resilience, and adapt intelligently. When we do so, we will individually and collectively gain ownership of our emotional state. We will learn that we can feel good without putting others down, without needing mind or body numbing substances, and without having to accept oppressive paradigms that put our personality and identities in a box. Science has given us the information and the tools; it's time we started using them.

In this book, you will learn you can bounce back and feel good again — or maybe, for the first time ever.

You may have noticed the spark in our logo. It represents the energy to bounce back. It's the spark in all of us that keeps us from giving up. It's the energy that brings joy and gets us moving, even when times are tough. Throughout our journey in this book, you will realize, this spark lives in you.

Introduction

Thank you for picking up this book. I'm grateful to have you as a reader, and I am excited to deliver on the promise of its title. But first, I need to take care of a few things.

Imagine this page is like the announcement before you get on an amusement park ride or airplane. Before we take off, please consider this important information.

1. WE ARE GOING TO TALK ABOUT REAL LIFE

That includes gentle discussions about difficult feelings and circumstances. For some of you, this might bring up memories or emotions. Please do two things while reading:

Stop. Take your time.

Reach out for help, especially if you're feeling overwhelmed.

We are going on a journey together, and I want you to enjoy it and feel invigorated and be excited for what you're going to experience. That's why I want you to start to practice our first powerful tool, just to get you in the mood. Don't worry, we will go deeper into techniques for getting calm, balanced, and feeling good. But, for now...

2. PRACTICE TAKING THE LONG BREATH

This breathing practice is deceptively easy, but it is a tool you can use any time you need to reset your body and emotions. Using it regularly will help you get grounded and balanced.

You'll learn how this tool works, along with many others, in *Chapter 3, Taming Your Nervous System.*

The Long Breath

Take a deep breath through your nose to the count of 6. Hold it for a moment.

Now, release it slowly out of your mouth to the count of 10.

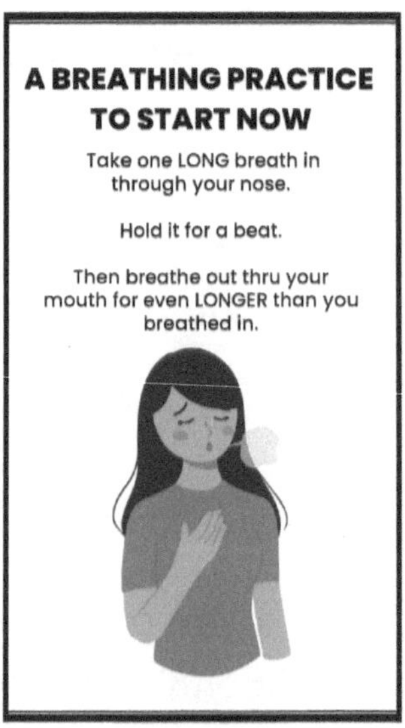

If you stretch or focus on relaxing your muscles before, during, or after the breath — that's a bonus move. Do one or two breaths as often as needed.

You may feel nothing at first, but most people feel a sense of calm in their mind and warm relaxation in their body. This may last for a moment or for hours.

If at any time you're feeling anxious,

depressed, confused, or just “out of it,” know that you’re not supposed to deal with these feelings alone. As you’ll learn, from a biological and evolutionary standpoint, we were built to need each other, support each other, and help each other heal. If you’re not sure where to get help, at the end of this book is a list of resources.

Also, if you're not feeling well, check in with your doctor. Everything from hormonal imbalances to physical illnesses can affect moods and emotions. So, see your doctor if things feel off. I'm sure you know this, but it is always worth repeating: Eat right, get enough sleep, and take time to relax. That's the foundational stuff. The deeper knowledge about how to feel good, you will learn in this book.

Before we begin, I want to share something personal.

I wrote this book for many reasons, but the primary one is this: I have spent decades working with people navigating profound adversity. Over and over again, I’ve seen how quickly we judge behavior when we don’t understand what’s underneath it. So called "dysfunctional" behaviors are not flaws, but adaptive responses.

If you are a young person living through a difficult childhood right now, or an adult still carrying the weight of one, this book is for you. I was one of those kids too.

So let’s begin.

Here’s the first thing you need to know:

It's not your fault.

1

It's Not Your Fault

You may not control all the events that happen to you, but you can decide not to be reduced by them.
– Maya Angelou

There is a lot about your life and your circumstances that just landed on you, and you're stuck dealing with the aftermath. If you have ever thought, "What did I do to deserve this?" as you stand with your arms outstretched in the middle of a mess, this chapter might blow your mind a bit.

The answer to "What did I do to deserve this?" is this: "Probably nothing." Much about you and your circumstances is simply *Not Your Fault.*

Quick story to illustrate my point.

It was 2006, and I was running a community development

agency that oversaw a low-income housing project in a crime-ridden part of San Francisco. One afternoon, I was in my third-floor office when a rock hit my window. I ran to see what happened.

Five boys, ages 10 to early teens, were in the parking lot below, laughing. When they saw me, they did an "oh shit!" and ran.

I sped down the stairs yelling, "I know who you are! I know your moms!" When I caught up to them, I told them the window would cost $300 to fix (this had happened before), and they needed to work it off. The rest of the day they spent weeding and sweeping the front of the building. I told them to come back in three days. I wanted to get to know them better.

Over snacks and a movie (*When We Were Kings*, about Muhammad Ali), I learned their stories. Obviously, they were growing up poor in a dangerous public housing neighborhood.

Most told me about dads who were missing in their lives, some of whom were incarcerated. They were being raised by mothers or grandmothers who were overworked, overwhelmed, or dealing with their own struggles. Their schools were uninspiring — when they actually went to school. Their dreams were to one day have a fat wallet, drive a nice car, maybe a black SUV with loudspeakers, and girls in the back. They were, in essence, typical "at-risk youth." I could see where they were headed.

I started a small after-school program to get them interested in learning more about themselves and to prepare them for better opportunities outside of the neighborhood. I didn't know how to help them, but I wanted them to see that they deserved to have successful, safe, and happy lives.

Long after I had left the job, I learned that one boy ended up in a wheelchair from a serious car accident. The leader of the group, a bright and charismatic kid, died by gunshot. I hope the others are doing well, but the odds are they are not living up to the potential they had. Even getting the nice car and fat bills probably never materialized. They deserved better.

After that experience, I have dedicated myself to understanding what makes some people succeed in fulfilling their lives, and others have to struggle so much, like those boys.

Their stories haunt me still. Those kids were set up for hard lives by forces beyond their control. It wasn't their fault. So much was lined up against them, and I guarantee that even if you're not a "kid from the projects," the same factors that were holding them back are affecting you too.

THE 5 FACTORS THAT SHAPE YOU

Before you ever made a single life choice, five big factors were already shaping your brain, body, and emotions:

YOUR NERVOUS SYSTEM: We will talk a lot more about your nervous system in *Chapter 3: Taming Your Nervous*

System. For now, just know that when people talk about their *nerves*, they are usually talking about their stress response, which includes fight or flight, along with freeze, fawn, and faint/collapse responses.

From an evolutionary standpoint, your nervous system was designed to keep you physically safe — without you having to think too much. Your mind and body are set up to just *react*.

How? Our nervous system is designed to *fight* off a predator or *flee* from one. It was designed to *freeze* your body so you can escape being detected by a predator. The *fawn* response tries to appease others so you're not a target (think of people-pleasing). Then there is the *faint* response, where you might pass out instead of having to go through something awful (an extreme response).

These are the classic "fight or flight" responses that live in us.

Bottom line: From an evolutionary standpoint, our "nerves" are set up to respond when things don't feel safe. They are automatic responses that hit before we are fully aware of what is causing us to feel fear or threat. That means our fight or flight responses are connected to feelings of fear, and are not under our conscious control.

The boys at my work were triggered all the time because they lived in an unsafe environment, with gunshots and other scary things always lurking in the background of their lives. This was just one of the 5 Factors that affected their childhoods.

YOUR GENETICS AND EPIGENETICS: You probably know that the color of your eyes and your height are determined by your genes. Genetic traits like being pretty, tall, or athletic can feel like an unfair advantage, and traits like physical disabilities, poor eyesight, or having bad teeth feel unfair. You had nothing to do with this process.

But there's another layer that acts like little chemical "switches" on your genes that turn certain traits up or down depending on what's happening in your life. That's epigenetics. If your great-great-grandmother survived a famine, you may carry epigenetic markers that cause you to hold on to calories. If your distant ancestor lived through wars and being alert to danger kept them alive, you may be prone to being anxious and hypervigilant to threats.

But if your life is less stressful, that trait can be turned down.

In other words, carrying a genetic trait does not guarantee it will be expressed. Living in a calm and supportive environment and keeping your nervous system regulated reduces the likelihood that certain stress-related genetic patterns become active.

That means that less stress and more safety in your life could influence future generations. You won't change the genes that you pass down, but you might shape how bodies develop and react in future generations.

Feeling good isn't selfish. You are a vital link in the ongoing evolution of future generations – and striving toward feeling good in ways that support healthy development is how we evolve.

The next of the 5 Factors shows why this is especially true.

INTERGENERATIONAL TRAUMA: Your family tree might include people who survived slavery, colonization, racism, war, genocide, or forced migration. You may come from a line of folks who faced addiction, violence, or untreated mental illness. Or maybe generations learned to shut down their emotions just to get through life.

Those survival strategies can leave marks in our bodies and minds. Part of this comes from epigenetics, and part comes from the coping habits we inherit by watching the people around us.

Families and communities pass down both helpful and harmful ways of dealing with life. For example, in some communities, neighbors support each other, and parents step in to help care for children. Others cope by isolating or using substances to numb out difficult feelings. We learn these patterns without even realizing it, and unless we become conscious of them, we can pass those same patterns to the next generation.

ADVERSE CHILDHOOD EXPERIENCES (ACEs): The landmark Kaiser ACE Study revealed that people who grow up with abuse, neglect, household dysfunction, or exposure to violence face a higher risk of serious health problems later in life. These include heart and lung disease, diabetes, kidney disease, and some cancers, as well as increased rates of depression, anxiety, substance use, and risky behaviors.

Clearly, none of us had control of the home conditions we were born into. Our childhood experiences may not have been healthy, appropriate, or caring. Sometimes it's because parents themselves are passing along their own childhood dysfunction to their children as part of their Intergenerational Trauma. Sometimes, difficult childhoods happen because a parent passes away, or suffers from health issues, or the family lives in a violent community they can't escape from.

Early childhood adverse experiences can have a lasting effect on us for three main and often overlapping reasons.

1. Chronic stress in childhood can influence how genes are expressed through epigenetic processes. See above.

2. Stress during key developmental times in a child's life can alter their brain development. The systems that are responsible for detecting danger, such as the amygdala (the part of our brain that detects danger and triggers our fight or flight response), may become more reactive. Meanwhile, the parts of the child's brain that regulate their emotions and help with decision-making and learning get disrupted.

Think of it this way: A child experiencing the stress of ACEs might need to develop a good threat detection system.

That means the parts of the brain that trigger their nervous system to protect them from abuse, neglect, household chaos, or violence, will take a front seat developmentally, while the parts of the brain that are open, curious, and ready to learn get held back.

If a child grows up never knowing when the next explosion of anger is coming, their brain can become highly tuned to and constantly scanning for threats. That same hyper-alertness can make it harder to focus on school, relax around new people, or develop trust.

3. When stress builds up we look for ways to cope that will help us feel good right away and at least temporarily. This can show up as tantrums and problems in school when kids are young. Kids then can get labeled as the "problem" and begin to see themselves that way, too.

As they get older it can include looking for relief through drugs or alcohol, thrill-seeking and impulsive behaviors, or ways that help them feel more in control of their environment.

Think of the child who is constantly moving, talking, doing "dumb," daring, dangerous things, or shutting down and going inward and being antisocial. These behaviors may be a sign that they are trying to distract themselves from their uncomfortable feelings.

Strategies that start out as coping responses or emotional distractions, like drug use, alcohol abuse, smoking, or seeking multiple sexual partners, can then lead to chronic health problems later in life.

The best way to look at the outcome of having a difficult childhood is that our brain and body are trying to stay safe and protected. When we don't have this fundamental need met, life gets dysfunctional.

THE ENVIRONMENT YOU LIVE IN: Do you live in a bad neighborhood? Do you live in a highly polluted area? A war-torn area? Are you a refugee struggling in a place where you're not accepted? Is your government oppressive? Are you living in a racist, sexist, or classist society?

Having to tiptoe through circumstances, never sure about whether you're going to be accepted, attacked, or ignored, will affect how you see your life. Our environment is the fishbowl we swim in. We think "this is just how things are" and don't realize how we may constantly feel unsafe.

You may notice two things about the 5 Factors:

1. They affect every single person on Earth, just in different ways.

2. They all come from one basic drive: We are all just trying to survive.

How many (if not all) of these factors play a role in who you are, and where you are, today?

Like most of us, you probably had some good things and

some not-so-good things come from the 5 Factors. They can work together, with some of the negatives balanced by the positives and vice versa. Maybe you had neglectful parents, but enjoyed a safe neighborhood, and you were gifted with a unique talent. Maybe your home life was idyllic, but you lived in a racist society and experienced deep poverty and discrimination.

We all get dealt a different hand of cards to play with in life. So blaming yourself because you're easily triggered to anger, or can't stop being anxious, or want to stay away from crowds, doesn't necessarily make sense, given the 5 Factors. *However...*

Despite everything: You Are the Winner of Evolution!

You must realize you are pretty extraordinary. You're the result of a long line of humans who managed to stay alive long enough to reproduce through harrowing and deadly times. You're the prime — the apex of our species. All of us, despite the things that set us back, are part of the genetic line of humans who made it to the 21st century.

So why can we feel so miserable if we've fought this valiant biological struggle to make it from primordial ooze to the tech-filled "let's go to space" and "we make smart machines" world we were born into?

The problem is that some of the nervous system settings that kept our ancestors alive may now be getting in our way.

Take the ACEs Test

Adverse Childhood Experiences (ACEs) are stressful events, like abuse, neglect, household dysfunction, or exposure to violence, that happen before age 18. The more ACEs you have, the more at-risk you may be for long-term health and behavior issues.

A high ACE score does *not* predict your future.

ACEs show what you've lived through so that you can trace back certain traits and behaviors you may have adopted in order to cope with your adversity. You can find a link to the ACEs Assessment in the Resources page at the end of this book.

WHY OUR NERVOUS SYSTEM FEELS OUT OF WHACK

We are built to deal with immediate physical threats; that's the gift of our nervous system. Given what our species has gone through over thousands of years, we are lucky to have evolved to be ready to fight off a neighboring tribe, outrun a tiger on the savanna, and keep our bodies alive when food is scarce. We adapted quite well.

But today, most of our stress comes from pressures that are ongoing and mostly invisible. If our evolutionary ancestors worried about a tiger chasing them, we worry about our to-do lists, bills to pay, and thoughts and fears about the future.

We're exposed to stressors our ancestors could never have imagined. We're hyper-connected to global and local crises like wars and injustices, and terrible events we can watch instantly on our screens. We compare our lives to perfectly curated Instagram images and feel constant pressure to succeed in a hyper-competitive, "winner-take-all" economy.

We're dealing with problems that are conceptual and chronic rather than immediate and physical. Our world evolved faster than our biology did.

Our troubles are different, so our responses must evolve and adapt too.

THE HAND YOU WERE DEALT

How are we supposed to deal with these 5 Factors that we had no control over?

For a long time, scientists thought the brain was pretty much done changing after childhood. One of the biggest discoveries in neuroscience has been the understanding that our brains continue to change. It's called *neuroplasticity.*

Neuroplasticity means your brain is constantly rewiring itself. Every time you practice a new skill, calm yourself instead of going off on someone, say something kind instead of being judgmental, or reach out for help instead of isolating yourself — you are literally carving a tiny new path in your brain.

If you keep at it, the path becomes a roadway, then a highway, until that new groove becomes your default setting.

Stanford neuroscientist Robert Sapolsky argues that biology, genetics, childhood experiences, and environment are so powerful that we don't have any free will at all. It's like living in the Matrix. We are preprogrammed into this life, and even the thought "I have free will" is just our brains fooling ourselves.

I don't know if he's right, but his research into the way our brains and bodies work is central to what I have just shown in *It's Not Your Fault*. The debate may go on about whether we have free will or are living in the Matrix. In the meantime, for purposes of your emotional evolution, the question remains:

How do you feel?

Do you feel more aware of yourself? Do you feel more hopeful? Do you feel connected to others? Do you have tools to feel good? Do you see your life as a story that matters?

Because how you experience your life is real to you. You're the player in, and the observer of, your life.

WHERE IS YOUR POWER?

Let's put this all together:

You didn't choose your nervous system settings.

You didn't choose your genes or your ancestors' trauma.

You didn't choose your childhood.

You didn't choose the big systems you were born into.

But you *do* get to choose what you do next with the nervous system you have, the beliefs you hold, the dreams you want to make into reality, and the skills and tools you operate with.

Feeling good starts with learning to turn down the alarm in your body. It means you have the power to rewrite your inner story — even get the things you missed getting when you were a child (you'll learn how to do this in the sections on the 6 Building Blocks for Resilience).

Feeling good also means you can spot when people are trying to manipulate you through fear. It means you can sustain a good relationship. It means feeling more delighted with your life and feeling a sense of meaning, creativity, and power.

Your next step is very important. To get to where you want to go, you need to know where you came from and what's holding you back. It takes a hero to live today with the nervous system we have and the world as it is.

Think about the 5 Factors and consider that they are where you started in life.

You're a hero. And every hero needs an Origin Story. The 5 Factors make up the elements of your Origin Story.

As the hero of your life, you are living a unique quest through your personal emotional evolution. Like many of us, you may be seeking answers to the most vital questions of all: *Why am I here? What am I meant to do? What's my path?*

Grab your backpack with the 5 Factors you were given in life, stick a hat on your head to protect you from the negative thoughts that will say "this won't work for me," and bravely step into the unknown.

Let's start your Hero's Journey.

2

You Are the Hero of Your Life

The hero's journey is a symbol that binds, in the original sense of the word, two distant ideas, the spiritual quest of the ancients with the modern search for identity. – Joseph Campbell

Whether you're struggling with something or just going through a blah period of your life, seeing yourself as a hero can give you a mental map to make sense of where you are now and where you're headed. Why do you need this? Because what makes us humans powerful is our ability to see ourselves as part of a larger story. It's the basis for our drive toward religions, our connections to our country, our ethnic identities, and other factors that give our lives context. But, it can also become easily manipulated. That's why we must become the authors of our own heroic journey.

How to tell the Story of You

The 5 Factors we discussed in *Chapter 1* — your nervous system, your genetics, generational trauma, Adverse Childhood Experiences, and your environment — can make you feel caged in by random things you can't control. But what if those difficult experiences aren't random?

What if they are the beginning of something?

Heroes usually start not knowing what they have inside of them. Something special. Then, something happens. It's the Hero's Origin Story, and it sets everything in motion. The 5 Factors that affect you are part of your Origin Story.

The historian Yuval Noah Harari says that what separates us from the chimpanzees (with whom we share 95% of our genetic makeup) is our capacity for storytelling.

We can talk about the science of feeling good, but stories make the science relevant to our lives. In this and the following chapters, I will use stories to illustrate the scientific principles I will share.

Stories are so powerful that they can determine how we live. If you frame your struggles as evidence that life is unfair and you're unlucky, you'll feel helpless and victimized.

If you frame those same struggles as the opening chapter of a Hero's Journey, suddenly your adversity has meaning.

One of my favorite stories illustrates how we interpret

what events in our lives mean. It's the classic Taoist fable called *The Chinese Farmer*. Here's how it goes:

A farmer's horse runs away. The neighbors come by to offer condolences and shake their heads: "What bad luck you have!" The farmer's reply is "Maybe."

The next day, the horse comes back and brings with him a herd of wild horses. The neighbors are a bit jealous: "What good fortune you have!" Again, the farmer replies, "Maybe."

The farmer's son tries to ride one of the wild horses, falls, and breaks his leg. The neighbors are sympathetic: "What terrible luck that is!" The farmer responds, "Maybe."

The next day, the emperor's army comes through the village conscripting young men for war. Because of his broken leg, the farmer's son isn't chosen. The neighbors again exclaim, “What good luck!” The farmer says, "Maybe."

How many times have you heard someone (or maybe even yourself) say, "That was a really rough experience, but it turned out to be the best thing that could have happened to me"?

On the other hand, maybe you got what you wanted, and it was the worst thing that could have happened (search *real-life lottery winners* to see my point). How you look at events can change your experience of them.

Like the farmer, you can withhold judgment about whether things are good or bad to allow new interpretations for the question *What just happened to me?*

YOUR LIFE IS A NOBLE QUEST

Throughout history, humans have told the same stories over and over. A classic one is about the hero who falls and then rises again against all odds.

These kinds of stories get repeated because they describe true-to-life patterns.

Your storyline may not be totally unique, and that's good news because they show others have walked the same path and found their way through. For those of you who are pattern recognition experts, you'll like where this is headed.

The Hero's Journey shows up in ancient myths, religious writings, and modern superhero movies. I'm a fan of those movies, so you'll have to forgive my ongoing references to them, but I find them to be fun examples of larger patterns in life.

The psychologist Carl Jung called these patterns *archetypes*. He considered them maps of the human psyche.

When my son was young, we read through a ton of books with archetypal stories: *The Hobbit*, *The Lord of the Rings*, *His Dark Materials*, the *Harry Potter* books, *The Hunger Games*, and even the *Little House on the Prairie* books offer archetypal vignettes.

If you identified with any of the characters, you're well

on your way to understanding the Hero's Journey. Same if you watched any of the *Star Wars*, *Dune*, *Marvel* or DC *Comics* movie franchises; their storylines follow the Hero's Journey template.

Many of the writers of these stories admit being inspired by the mythologist Joseph Campbell, who mapped out a far more complex and detailed spiritual Hero's Journey than we will work with here.

For our purposes, I've created a simpler version.

YOUR HERO'S JOURNEY TEMPLATE

Origin Story: The traumatic beginnings of your journey. These can include your 5 Factors, or other events.

Unknown Powers and Secrets: Things that weren't right about your life, and/or hidden powers you believed you had, but didn't feel safe revealing yet.

Mentor or Sidekick: Someone you could confide in and trust with your secrets, or someone who became a helpful guide.

Kryptonite: The things that sap your power. Like bad habits, addictions, or negative thought patterns. These are things you have to learn to avoid or overcome.

Honing Your Superpower: The period where you build up your powers, learn to manage them, and gain confidence in using them.

Who Do You Save?: The moment you feel ready to use your powers and you know you can make a difference. It might be saving yourself, your family, or someone going through the same Origin Story you went through.

Story: Tina's Hero's Journey

Here's an example. Follow Tina, a 34-year-old, on her Hero's Journey after she discovered she couldn't have children.

Origin Story: Tina had several miscarriages throughout her relationship with Samuel. Her doctors couldn't explain why, but she was unable to carry a baby to term. It was just something she was born with. Her sadness and tension about not being able to be a mother weighed on their relationship, and she and Samuel split up.

Secrets She Kept: After her first miscarriage, Tina had a premonition that she would never be able to have children or get married. This feeling was so strong that she spent over a decade secretly believing she was doomed. Something was wrong with her.

Mentor/Sidekick: In her late 20s, Tina's good friend Christy got pregnant during a short relationship with a man who moved away a few months later. During long walks and talks, Tina tried to convince Christy to keep the child and not, as she was considering, give it up for adoption. Tina was so passionate in her arguments that Christy could keep the baby and be a good single mother that one day Christy turned to Tina and said, "If you think it's such a good idea and so 'doable' to be a single parent ... why don't you adopt a child and do it yourself?"

Kryptonite: Tina realized it was easy for her to tell Christy to "go it alone." But Christy wasn't ready to be a mother. Both Christy and Tina liked to go out late and they probably drank a bit too much; they both smoked. They were enjoying being free of too many responsibilities. Plus, Tina was a downer. She wasn't the most positive person. She was anxious and lived on "bad feelings" and premonitions that her life wasn't going to turn out well. Tina realized she had become cynical and dark.

Honing her Superpowers: After that conversation with Christy, Tina decided to move to a different town, where there was less partying, and where she could enjoy more sunlight and fresh air. Then Tina got serious about money. She saved enough to move to a small condo, a place she could make her own.

She got a dog so she could learn what it means to take care of something other than herself. She worked on her attitude. Things *could* get better, she told herself. There were many ways to find love and family, and as a modern woman, she had choices! Based on her optimism, Tina applied to become a foster parent. She did the work, taking classes and putting her life in order so she could become certified to have a child placed with her.

She was scared but did it anyway.

Who Do You Save?: Tina saved herself from a life of negative beliefs about her future. She focused on what mattered to her, sharing what she had, and believing she could be a mother. Within six months of being a foster parent, a baby girl was placed in her home. She eventually adopted that child, and they became the family Tina never thought she could have.

Over the years, Tina inspired several other women with similar situations to adopt babies on their own, and they became a close group of friends with adopted kids.

Later in this book, in the Storytelling Building Block chapter, you'll have an opportunity to map out your own Hero's Journey using this template. Or, if you're ready, you can try it now by going to *Chapter* 12.

THE BRAIN SCIENCE BEHIND THE HERO'S JOURNEY

When you speak positively to yourself, like saying, "I'm heroically going through this tough situation," your brain releases dopamine, the brain chemical for motivation and reward. This small burst tells your nervous system, "You're safe. Carry forth!" That signal lowers your fight-or-flight while also increasing courageous feelings. It's not a magical potion that will change everything, but it is part of a process, a pattern you can start to build where you're reducing the sense of threat and increasing your sense of power.

That's why just saying, "I am the hero of my life," as I asked you to do at the beginning of this chapter, can start you on your path to feeling good.

The stories we tell about ourselves can also activate neural pathways in our brains. When you're on a Hero's Journey, your brain will build new connections that help you see yourself differently. Every time you say, "I'm a hero," you're doing some magic up there in your noggin, connecting new wiring.

Frame yourself as a victim, and your brain says, "OK, you're a victim."

Frame yourself as a hero, and your brain starts building power.

YOUR BODY DOESN'T KNOW IT'S A HERO YET BECAUSE IT IS AFRAID

There is a book, now considered a classic in psychology circles, about how trauma affects our bodies. It's called *The Body Keeps the Score.* The author, psychiatrist and researcher Bessel van der Kolk, found that stress and trauma are held in our bodies, not just our minds and emotions. To help people with Post-Traumatic Stress Disorder (PTSD), we must incorporate the body, which keeps a "score" of what has happened to us.

That score can show up as patterns the body learns when it has had to face danger. These patterns include how we feel, how we react, the hormones that are released, how our muscles tense, the way we breathe, and how our nervous system responds.

In other words, the body remembers how you survived something frightening, but it doesn't always connect what it's experiencing now with the facts of what actually happened in the past.

A classic example comes from people returning from war. They were once labeled "shell-shocked." A car engine backfiring, the sound of a helicopter, or fireworks going off could send a former soldier's body back to the moment of battle. If they once ran, crouched, covered their head, or shouted, their body might respond the same way years later, even in a completely different setting.

A simple way to understand this is that the body is constantly asking: *Was I safe?* If the answer was no, it may store the memory of the reaction without storing the context. This is why we might overreact when a fearful memory from the past connects to a comment, a raised hand, a threatening tone of voice, or someone standing too close behind us. Our body remembers and wants to re-enact what happened.

Van der Kolk emphasizes that insights we gain through, for example, talk therapy won't always get to the bottom of why we react to certain events the way we do. Healing must involve restoring bodily awareness and safety. Working with the body helps release the trauma response. Some healing practices that work are:

Breath regulation

Yoga and mindful movement

EMDR (a therapy that uses eye movement while processing memory)

Rhythmic activity like dance or drumming

Play and creative therapies, even for adults — using miniatures in a sandbox can help in reprocessing

The point is not simply to "talk it out," but to help the nervous system relearn what it feels like to be safe.

Let's take this idea and apply it to everyday hardships, disappointments, and stressors.

Let's say you've just gotten terrible news. The college you dreamed of attending your whole life just rejected your application, or your dream job went to someone else. This isn't "trauma" like almost getting hit by an IED. But it is a shock of sorts.

You may automatically feel your shoulders slump. Your chest collapses. You look down. Your body feels heavy, as if it's carrying the weight of what just happened.

Then, the emotions hit: fear, dread, embarrassment, guilt, shame, or anger.

Then the thoughts show up: *I'm a failure. Everything is stacked against me!*

Here's what's happening biologically:

The brain's threat detection systems activate first. Your body shifts into fight or flight mode. Emotions rise along-side those shifts. Then your thinking mind interprets what the event means to you.

The reaction happens so fast, it's often faster than our awareness. It may feel like you "felt bad" first, but physiologically, the body and emotional systems were already fired up.

If often feels like the opposite, doesn't it? You got the bad news, you felt emotional, had negative thoughts about what it meant, then you noticed your body felt tired, achy, or jittery.

The point of seeing yourself as a hero is to have something to do after the bad news hits, and once your nervous system has had a moment to settle down a bit. Can you put yourself into a heroic framework?

In real life, this might look like researching new schools, finding a different job, or stepping back to assess what your next move will be. Bessel van Der Kolk tells us that if we want to avoid having these emotional and physical states get lodged in us, we need to release the tension from our bodies so that it doesn't get stuck in a pattern.

With a heroic perspective, how would you reset your body?

Think about how you might carry yourself. Would your shoulders slump and your feet shuffle around zombie-like? Or would you lift your head, take in the situation, and start planning your next move? I like to imagine myself as a squinty-eyed superhero, surveying the scene, gathering information, and deciding what to do next.

That rejection notice can become your Origin Story moment. It's the event that pushes you to reapply, retool, or retrain. You can then look at your emotional reaction with some objectivity. Does this moment really call for you to feel shame, anger, or despair? If it does, that's OK. But as a hero, you know you can't sit in those feelings without losing your powers.

You might see yourself in the *Honing Your Superpower* phase. In movies, this is the montage where the superhero crashes while learning to fly, their tools malfunction, or they try to fight before their energy is fully restored. You're allowed to fail and get up. That is, in essence, the Hero's Journey. Progress is often awkward, and you need to focus on the classic hero quote, "Whatever you do, don't give up!"

This isn’t about denying your feelings of disappointment. The rejection still hurts. But the meaning changes, and meaning influences how you think, how you feel, and even how you hold your body. You want to *physically feel* like a hero.

It means experimenting with what's called *embodiment*, which simply means your brain, body, sensations, and emotions are linked. Maybe you stand taller. Maybe you plant your feet more firmly. There’s a posture called a *command pose*, sometimes referred to as the *Wonder Woman pose*: standing with your feet apart and your hands on your hips. Try it. See if you notice how shifting your body can subtly shift your mental state.

The point of embodiment is to interrupt automatic survival patterns and consciously reset how your body responds to a challenge. Over time, this can help you gain greater ownership of your physical, mental, and emotional states.

In the next chapter, we'll go deeper into releasing tension from the body. For now, follow the steps to notice your emotions, reset your thinking, and try to strike a new pose.

HEROES VS. BULLIES

You may have just read the previous section and felt like no matter how you stand or what you say to yourself, you've had to deal with bullies and mean people all of your life. You don't feel heroically powerful.

Let's talk about bullies – the villains of the heroic struggle. Being a hero is about finding your internal, authentic strength and power.

Bullying is about trying to strip you of your powers.

Bullies come in many flavors. There's the old school tough guy/girl bully, who blocks your way, won't let you get to your locker, and tries to trip you or knock things out of your hands.

There's the emotional bully, whispering mean things to you to make you feel sad and flustered.

The mean girl/guy bully is about making sure you are left out of the group, and *they* are the ones who decide whether you are accepted.

This isn't just about memories of annoying middle school pests. Bosses or any other people who control aspects of your life (such as money, time, or privileges) can be bullies.

Politicians, religious leaders, teachers, and business leaders can be bullies. They cause a tremendous amount of suffering and are often part of what makes up the "Environment" of the *It's Not Your Fault* Environment Factor.

What Makes a Bully?

Bullying behavior often begins with the *bully* experiencing nervous system dysregulation. When someone experiences chronic internal feelings of threat, and fight or flight feelings kick in, those feelings can be uncomfortable to sit in.

Feelings like fear, shame, or insecurity can overwhelm the bully, and the bully uses dominance to try to relieve that discomfort.

A bully is anyone who uses aggressive verbal, physical, and control tactics to feel powerful at your expense.

Here is the key to understanding bullies: People who feel authentically good and in command of their own personal power do not need to bully.

That means that a bully is internally struggling to feel powerful — and they are using their interaction with you to get that feeling.

Here are some examples:

- The father who controls his children fears he is not in control of his life.
- The guy at the bar who goes off on someone for simply looking at him the wrong way is afraid of people.
- The mean girl who makes fun of the other girls' outfits is herself constantly worried about how she looks.

You can fill in the blanks for what might be making the bully in your life afraid. But I guarantee anyone who has to "punch down" to feel special and in control is deeply troubled and fearful. Bullies are, at their core, very insecure people.

Now, I don't say this so you feel sorry for them. Their insecurities are their issues to deal with.

I tell you so you can protect yourself.

HOW YOUR NERVOUS SYSTEM CAN BE HIJACKED

Over the past several years, it's become clearer to me how our nervous system can get manipulated. I see how advertisements, political movements, cults, and even religious organizations can gain access to our emotions by understanding how our nervous system works.

We've talked about how we switch from being afraid to feeling safe. Our nervous system scans for danger, gets ready to act, and then comes back down to safety. Anyone who understands this can use that information. It's not always used for nefarious purposes, but it can be.

That's why I want to point out the steps, because once you see how you're being influenced, you won't be able to unsee it. You will forever be aware (and wary) of how your nervous system can be hijacked.

Let me show you how I think it is done. See if you notice these steps in social movements, advertisements, and politics:

Step 1: Make People Feel Special

First, create a sense of belonging and recognition.

The people who do this are what we will call the Manipulators. The Manipulators tell people they are special, chosen, or unique and valuable. This is often based on characteristics those people had nothing to do with: where they were born, what they look like, what language they speak, or the group they belong to.

At a nervous-system level, this feels good. Being seen and valued activates the parts of our brain that seek to be rewarded for who we are and the parts of us that want to belong to a group. For someone who has felt ignored, powerless, or unseen, this can feel like finally coming home, that they've found "my people."

Step 2: Make Them More Special Than the "Others"

Next, the Manipulators might introduce some comparison. The message shifts from *you matter* to *you matter more.*

The Manipulators portray your group as superior, more deserving, more moral, more righteous than others. There is now an "us" and a "them." Another way to say "them" is "the Others."

This step often creates a mix of pleasure and tension. There's pride and belonging, but also a message from the Manipulators to be on alert: Those Others are different, so maybe they aren't to be trusted. That gets the nervous system on alert, scanning for threats. Someone is coming to take your special status away from you. "You don't want those Others to step into your circle of specialness," the Manipulators warn us.

People may not feel afraid yet, but the seeds have been planted.

Step 3: Introduce the Threat

Next comes fear.

The Manipulators portray the Others as taking something: your safety, your jobs, your children, your culture, your future. They are framed as dangerous, as immoral, or as invaders. They are taking your place!

At this point, stress responses are activated. Feelings like anger, anxiety, disgust, and hyper-alertness are natural and expected when someone is threatening us. Our body prepares to defend our specialness from people who will come to destroy us, our way of life, and our values. This becomes a replacement for thinking through problems that can be very complex. It becomes a very simple us vs. them situation. This is an uncomfortable feeling and needs relief, and the Manipulators know this.

Step 4: Offer Protection, Justice, or Retribution

The Manipulators say, "I/we will save you!" and it sounds great when you're afraid of the Others. Now a leader, a movement, a belief system, a product, or a brand is there to be your protector. *Only we can keep you safe. Only I can fix this. Stand with us, and you'll be protected.*

When we realize we are going to be protected, it's such a surge of relief. We get feelings of being connected and part of the tribe. Now our brain is registering that we are safe again.

But that safety is based on something outside of ourselves. It may rely upon our loyalty, or on blind belief in something or someone.

We can go from feeling good to feeling good with a little tinge of fear or doubt, then into fear, and then back to feeling good and safe. It's a simple cycle.

How would a hero handle the Manipulators?

Great heroes know that in every villain is a mirror to their darker selves, and even allies can turn on you. That's why heroes will try to seek justice, rules, and order instead of just satisfying personal vendettas.

Safety also comes from knowing your identity. A hero stays vigilant to guard their personal powers from lies and manipulation, and looks for protection from systems based on fairness and equity.

When you don't understand your nervous system, fear tactics can feel like they are reality. Feeling relief can feel like you're safe, and now you owe that feeling to someone or something. Being part of the group or tribe can feel like love and connection, even when it may mean you have to hold back questions, curiosity, compassion, or critical thinking (think of cult tactics). That's why everyone should learn nervous system basics, which we will dive into fully in the next chapter.

But when you *do* understand how fear and safety work in your body, something powerful happens. You can pause. You can notice when your emotions are being pushed and pulled. You can ask yourself, "*Is this actually making me safer, or am I being manipulated?*"

That pause is heroic behavior. In the next chapter, you'll learn about how to use something I call the *Charismatic Pause* to shake off the potential for being manipulated or having your nervous system hijacked.

> The Lure of Horror Movies and Jump Scares
>
> Some people love scary movies, especially the ones with intense jump scares. Video games and roller coasters do this too. It might be mimicking a part of the same nervous system manipulation process I've described above, but in a fun way:
>
> You're at the theater waiting for *that scene* everyone is talking about. It's 10 minutes into the movie. Suddenly, a Stranger in a white mask comes out of the shadows, and you practically leap out of your chair. A few seconds later, you laugh. They got you. You jumped. But you're OK. It's just a movie!
>
> Your brain loves that feeling of returning to safety after being afraid. Once again, you've made it and kept yourself alive.

HOW WE PROTECT OURSELVES FROM BULLIES

According to a recent global study on bullying, more than 30% of kids 12-17 are currently experiencing bullying. That 30% of kids will grow up and become adults who have been bullied, and they may experience being bullied as adults too. That means a significant percentage of people know what it feels like to be bullied. So, how should we, as youth or adults, deal with bullying?

First, I do not recommend dealing with a bully alone because 1) they chose you because they thought they could feel powerful over you. If you try to take them on yourself and you lose, you feed their sense of power; and 2) because when you bring other people in, you unbalance what they think is a power dynamic in their favor.

Whether the bully is the kid at your school, your boss, or your significant other, you want to reach out to others. Let people know what you've been going through. Ask for help to support you, even if it is just to have someone to talk to and be aware of the pressure you're under.

The next thing you must do is to "appeal to a higher authority." Because bullying is about power, you need to find ways to boost your power dynamic with them. If it's the kid at school, tell your parents, tell your teacher, tell your counselor, tell the principal. Each person has the capacity to do something, and should do something.

Go up the chain of command. Do not let "no snitching" stop you. "No snitching" was invented by bullies to keep "higher authorities" from coming in and stopping what they are doing.

In some neighborhoods, officials like the police may not be seen as a trusted "higher authority," and then you want to go to your trusted community leaders in religious, educational, and other organizations that can help protect you. If you can, recruit others to safely help you deal with the bully in your life.

For many of us, we feel that larger forces like politicians and businesses bully us by imposing laws, monopolizing what we can buy, or controlling our lives in other crucial ways. That's where, time and again, banding with others to vote, march and protest, call and complain in large numbers, can make a huge difference. If you think a business is a big polluter, or is unfair to its workers, or is jacking up prices "because we can," you can boycott that business and use your voice to let others know to avoid them. Same for corrupt politicians, bad landlords, or unfair local zoning laws. We have collective power to make change toward a more fair power-balanced world.

WHAT IF YOU ARE THE BULLY?

You may have read this section and realized you've been the bully.

Bullying is a pattern of human behavior and is an instinct many carry to try to feel less vulnerable. Once you recognize yourself as the bully, you will need to look inward to find out what is making you feel so powerless and insecure. Did someone bully you in the past? Are you struggling with feelings you don't understand? Did you learn this behavior from others? Does life feel uncontrollable, and bullying helps you feel like you can manage it better?

Your bullying is trying to mask unhappiness, and you may need to seek help to get to the bottom of those feelings. Bullying is like any short-term high; it feels good for a moment, and then you crash and need more. You need to feed that part of you that feels awful and that you're trying to hide from.

If you are a bully and feel no remorse, you may want to find out if you have narcissistic, sociopathic, or psychopathic tendencies. I'm not trying to insult you or make you feel bad. These traits are fairly rare and are thought to be largely influenced by genetics and can be epigenetic (switched on through stress or adverse childhood experiences). They can be part of things that are *Not Your Fault.*

As we learned, though, you can manage and even change many things that fall under that category, whether it's a genetic inclination or needing to heal from past trauma like ACEs. Many people with these conditions seek help to understand themselves better and to manage their behaviors so they do not hurt themselves or others. They report that doing so makes their lives feel more manageable and happier.

You've just learned how to reframe your story. You're learning about power dynamics. You're starting to try on the idea that you're the hero of your own journey, but your body may not be ready to run headlong into the fray.

As we've talked about, your nerves play a big role in

how you're going to respond to life. This requires self-knowledge. It's hard to feel heroic when your mind and body feel shaky and uncertain. Every hero must learn to face fear. The question is: how?

We face fear by understanding our nervous system's reactions to fear. That's what we are going to talk about in the next chapter.

How do we tame our nerves?

3
Taming Your Nervous System

Fear is the mind-killer. Fear is the little death that brings total obliteration. I will face my fear. I will permit it to pass over me and through me. — Bene Gesserit litany against fear, from "Dune" by Frank Herbert

FEAR IS YOUR BODY'S FIRST REACTION

Let me take you back in time. You're standing in a jungle thousands of years ago, gripping a roughly made spear. You haven't eaten in two days. The cave you left behind is cold. Your body is weak. Suddenly, you hear a roar. The bushes rustle. You freeze, heart pounding, your breathing shallow. A tiger emerges with yellow eyes locked on you. Energy floods your body. You hurl your spear. You miss! The tiger lunges. You turn and run, legs pumping, lungs burning.

You don't think. You just run.

Today, your brain and body are treating whatever is triggering your fear response like it's that ancient tiger and you're on the brink of personal extinction. We can get the same kinds of intense feelings rising up from someone taking the parking space we were patiently waiting for, *With Our Blinker On!* Something inside surges, and you're left feeling antsy and ready to do *something*: Fight, Flight, Freeze?

I have never met a tiger in the wild. But I have met a pile of past due bills I couldn't pay. I've been stranded on a dark, deserted highway with no gas and a stranger knocking on my car window telling me to open my door. I've overheard a workmate spreading mean gossip about me. I remember on each of those occasions feeling my heart rate rising, my brain getting scrambled, even feeling a little sick to my stomach after, because those things were upsetting.

Our bodies release a cascade of responses when we're afraid. It's a way of getting us ready to do what needs to get done to protect ourselves.

Fear gets our nervous system to respond physically: We feel ready to fight (*I'll punch my way through this problem*), to flee (*I'll run away*), to freeze (*Maybe it won't see me?*), to fawn (*If I say yes, maybe they'll leave me alone?*), to faint or collapse (*I can't deal with this right now, I'm shutting down*).

This physical response is not waiting for our brain to sort through options; it just wants to act, and act fast. It wants to do whatever is necessary to keep us alive.

Today, a lot of our problems are more conceptual than concrete, meaning they're problems we anticipate even before they arrive. Your body's alarm keeps going off for problems it can't physically fight, flee, or fix.

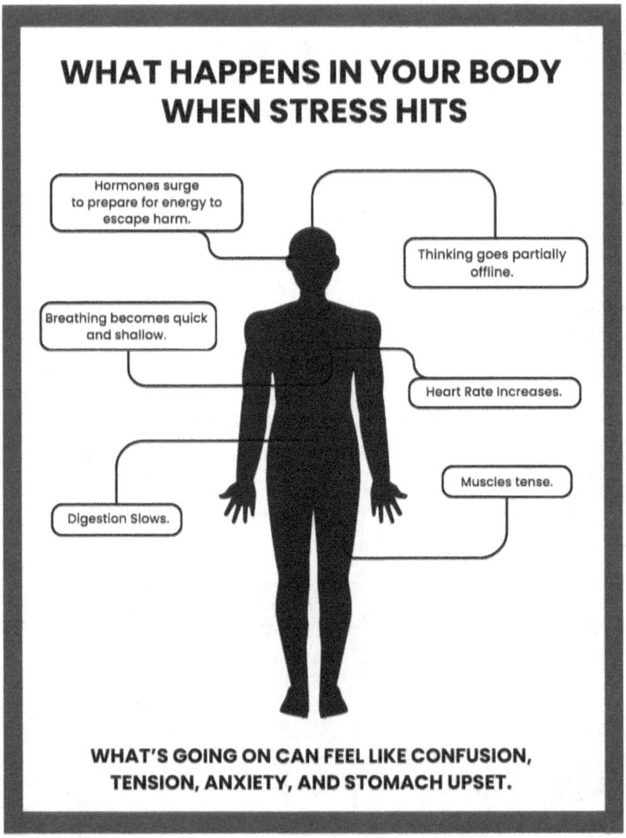

This physical response is not waiting for our brain to sort through options; it just wants to act, and act fast. It wants to do whatever is necessary to keep us alive.

Think of your brain as a building with a built-in alarm system. The part of the brain called the limbic system is the control room, always running in the background and deciding whether things feel safe or threatening. Inside that system is the amygdala — your alarm bell.

The amygdala's job is simple and fast: detect danger and react immediately. It doesn't stop to analyze or fact-check what's happening. If something reminds it of past fear, stress, or danger, it sounds the alarm.

Another part of the brain, the hippocampus, helps catalog and remember what felt threatening, so the system can be even more prepared next time. It's our own built-in security system and it is pretty amazing.

From an evolutionary standpoint, this alarm system has been very good at keeping our species alive. But on an individual level, it may not work well in every situation.

The problem is our alarm system isn't great at distinguishing between real danger and complex emotional stressors.

Let me give you an example: Let's say you're riding your bike down the street and suddenly someone opens their car door right in front of you. Your body is going to react instinctively to try to avoid crashing into it.

Let's say that you swerve and expertly avoid the open car door. Then, next block down, you ride by the person who just broke up with you.

Your alarm system has now been triggered again. You're feeling intense emotions like embarrassment, rejection, anger, or lack of control (maybe all at the same time!). Your body's alarm will go off like you're in serious trouble even when nothing terrible is actually happening.

As you ride by, your alarm is blaring and your body is getting worked up for fight or flight. Also, your thinking brain shuts down for a moment.

Oh no. Your ex saw you. They are waving "Hi!" Your limbs feel frozen. You can't talk and you feel flustered.

Learning how to calm the alarm through breathing, movement, and self-talk can help bring your thinking brain back online, and you can choose what to do next. As you near your ex, you take a deep breath. You talk to yourself, *I'm fine, I'm looking great today, and I feel good about us not being together.*

The fact that you're on your bike means your limbs are easier to loosen up. You pump your pedals to ride over. You stop for a sec, and you're now able to coolly respond: "Hey, it's good to see you!" You smile, chat for a minute, and say, "I'm late for this thing," and you wave goodbye as you ride your bike confidently into the sunset.

Instead of stammering or rushing off, pretending you didn't see them, you were able to decide how you wanted to respond in a way that made you feel good.

You were not at the mercy of your nervous system.

WHAT HAPPENS IN YOUR BODY WHEN STRESS HITS

Your body reacts before you have time to think about it. It starts a chain reaction:

1. The Alarm Goes Off: A small, ancient part of your brain called the amygdala scans for danger.
2. Chemicals Flood the System: Your brain signals the release of stress chemicals like adrenaline and cortisol.
3. Body Systems Shift into Survival Mode
    - Heart rate increases to pump blood to muscles
    - Breathing speeds up to bring in more oxygen
    - Muscles tense to prepare for action
    - Digestion slows or shuts down
4. Higher Thinking Goes Offline

Blood flow and energy are pulled away from the parts of the brain responsible for complex thought and language. That's why stress can make it harder to think clearly, consider your options, and stay calm or articulate in conversations.

EVOLUTION V. EXTINCTION

Our chronic stress response creates personal discomfort that needs release and relief. On a collective scale, being perpetually on edge for our survival can fuel animosity and even hatred toward others. When we feel insecure and vulnerable, we often look outward for someone to blame. We may point the finger at those we perceive as weaker to feel stronger ourselves, as we learned in the last chapter on bullying.

At a species level, this impulse can harden into rigid identities and ideologies meant to create a sense of safety. This desire for group safety was the genesis for the development of the tribe.

That tribe mentality has led to many "tribal" replacements, from small cultish groups to larger religious, political, and ideological movements. From the gang in the projects to NATO, we try to find safety in numbers.

There is nothing inherently wrong with seeking our tribe, except when tribal identity seeks to assert superiority and dominance over others. Then, our desire for safety can sometimes escalate into cruel politics and horrific wars.

Scratch beneath bigotry, nationalism, and feelings of class superiority, and we often find fear. (We will delve into this concept more in the *Belonging Building Block* chapter.)

However, superiority is not strength; it is a mask. The unspoken logic sounds something like this: *If I can domi-*

nate them, I will stay on top. If I stay on top, nothing can hurt me. Whether expressed defensively to protect what we have, or aggressively to protect what we fear losing, these behaviors can be attempts to manage fear and insecurity that are rooted in our ancient nervous system.

If we want to evolve and have any real hope of personal or global harmony, we have to learn how to manage our nervous systems more skillfully. Whether it's on the highway or at the negotiating table, we need tools that help us slow down and regain balance.

Part of the process of feeling good is allowing the nervous system to do what it is designed to do: detect potential danger and sound the alarm. That alarm is automatic. What is uniquely human is our capacity to pause, reinterpret what the alarm means (storytelling), and choose a response rather than an over-the-top reaction.

This is where our ability to talk to ourselves and reframe the story (like the Chinese Farmer) comes in. We can ask, *What does this event actually mean to me?* Our capacity for self-reflection, or storytelling, is key to our evolution. Failing to use it may be the cause of our extinction.

When we feel the urge to dominate, to lash out at a stranger behind a store counter, or to escalate conflict on a global scale, we need to ask: *can we find other ways to manage our fear of losing power or identity?* We must stop reacting out of the need for dominance and find ways to tap into our emotional intelligence and the parts of our minds that can creatively seek solutions. Heroic energy seeks harmony and gets into problem-solving mode, something humans can be very good at.

We just need to learn the tools and practice them.

WHEN FEAR BECOMES A PERSONALITY TRAIT

Our nervous system habits are the subconscious reactions we have to things that feel unsafe. Sometimes the threats are real: a truck is about to hit you as you cross the street, a snarling dog is running toward you with bared teeth, or you get a call that your child has had an accident and is in the hospital.

We need our nervous system ready to respond in these moments. But if we stay in constant alert mode without recovery time, we risk serious long-term mental, emotional, and physical health problems.

If unresolved stress isn't released, it can even become part of our personality.

Think about whether you have a go-to stress response. I used to go for a fight response for practically everything that happened. I was ready to talk mean, get in your face, and verbally punch my way through a problem.

Now, as I try to "evolve" my response, I take a moment, leave the situation, and try to release it through breathing and movement (walking, stretching, and talking myself down usually work for me). It's all a work in progress.

Your "go-to" nervous system response can start to feel like a personality trait, but it's just a learned pattern of protection. I often think of this when I see someone acting out in public. Like a "Karen." Think how differently we might see their behavior if we saw it as an unresolved stress response? Mind you, this is no excuse for bad behavior, but it can give us insight into why people act the way they do.

Some ways to look at personality as unresolved stress responses:

Fight: "You better compliment Betty's dinner or she will get in your face and accuse you of being ungrateful."

Flight: "When things get tough, Colin ghosts me for a few days."

Freeze: "Mai can't decide anything. She'd rather shut down than make a decision."

Fawn: "Roshandra says 'yes' to everyone just to keep the peace."

Faint/Collapse: "Roy has been known to take a 12-hour 'nap' when life gets too intense."

Note: *The faint response is concerning, especially if you literally pass out. It is usually an extreme reaction to high levels of stress and trauma.*

We need our nervous system ready to respond to real

threats. But if we stay in constant alert mode without recovery time, it takes a toll on our health.

One great visual to think of is that your body is like a car, and when your nervous system gets ready for fight or flight, it's like the car is getting revved up — like a race car ready for the start. If it doesn't have a race to run, it'll just sit there, revving. Think of what that would do to your car. Now think of what that does to your body.

KNOW YOUR TRIGGERS

It's important to understand what events trigger your nervous system reactions. When the threat is obvious and physical, your response makes sense. But you may have noticed that certain situations spark intense nervous system responses, even when you can't understand why.

Here's a personal story.

I spent quite a bit of time avoiding freeways when I lived in Los Angeles back in the day. Freeways made me nervous. I would inevitably have an anxiety attack, which felt like the freeze response taking over.

Of course, you can't freeze while driving. I had to concentrate on continuing to breathe as my heart raced, my hands gripped the steering wheel, and my vision hyper-focused on the car in front of me. Freeways were my trigger.

It took time to unravel what was happening. I was 17 and

living on my own with an apartment, a job, bills to pay, and older men asking me out for dates. I felt unsure about how to exist in an adult world while still feeling like a high school student. Everything felt overwhelming.

One day, I was talking to a friend and said, "I feel like everything goes too fast. It's all coming at me at once, and I feel like if I focus on one thing, the other things will crash into me." When I heard myself say those words, the connection clicked.

Take my statement "It's all coming at me too fast ... crash into me," and think about what a fast, aggressive L.A. freeway feels like. My brain had made a conceptual, symbolic connection: My life felt like a crazy, out-of-control drive down a freeway.

I didn't stop being nervous on the freeway immediately, but I did notice I could do things to feel more comfortable, like avoid certain times, stay in the slow lane, or follow a car that seemed to be driving normally. Eventually, my triggered anxiety dropped away.

To this day, I'm not afraid to drive on a freeway. (I might still get annoyed, though. Hello, fight response!)

Here's what fascinates me about triggers: They're often symbolic.

My life was like a crazy, chaotic, can't-get-off-the-freeway energy. Maybe the smell of toasting bread connects you to the day you were making breakfast and you got a phone call with bad news. Now, burnt toast sends you on a vague anxiety spiral. We all have our triggers, which our creative brain can turn into connections that are poetic in their symbolism. Once I got negative health news and when I did I looked down at my hands. I was wearing orange fingernail polish. To this day, I will not wear that color.

To find your triggers, ask yourself:

What situations make my heart race even though I'm not in physical danger?

What reminds me of times I felt powerless or unsafe?

When do I react more strongly than the situation seems to warrant?

Your triggers are usually connections your brain made between past pain and present circumstances. You won't be able to eliminate all triggers. Nor would you want to. They are often notifications to be aware of and heed.

What you want to do, once you know what your triggers are, is to learn how to guide your nervous system back to safety. If the trigger is real, you will have the energy to do what you need to do – like run or fight. If it's more conceptual and not really putting you in danger, you still need to release unused energy (like a gazelle in the wild releases its pent-up energy with a full-body shiver).

When you allow yourself to get out of the "survival state," you can more quickly get to the "rest and recovery state."

That helps reduce the wear and tear on your body, mind, and emotions.

WORKING WITH YOUR NERVOUS SYSTEM

Think of it as emotional aikido. You aren't fighting your reactions; you are redirecting their energies.

When you begin to notice your physical cues, like your racing heart, tight chest, and shallow breathing, don't label them as "bad" reactions. They're protective. Your body is your friend!

The trick is learning how to help it finish the job and move into recovery instead of getting stuck in survival mode.

The Fire and the Paramedics

Your nervous system has *two* main gears. The *sympathetic nervous system* is your body's accelerator. It fires you up to respond to danger or challenge. It releases adrenaline and cortisol so you can run, fight, or freeze.

Then there's the *parasympathetic nervous system*, which I think of as like paramedics coming to the rescue. Its job is to slow everything down once the threat has passed, lowering your heart rate, relaxing your muscles, restoring your digestion, and calming your mind and body (also known as "rest-and-digest" mode).

Think of it like this: The sympathetic system lights the fire, and the parasympathetic system sends the paramedics to the rescue.

When you recognize that your body has both systems, you can stop seeing fear as your enemy. Fear is simply your body's fire alarm alerting you to possible danger. What we're learning to do is not disable the alarm but to make sure we can reset it when it goes off unnecessarily.

Here's a quick guide to ways you can support your body so you can get to the recovery feel-good phase faster:

FIGHT: Release energy safely. Breathe out twice as long as you breathe in, shake out your limbs, or splash cold water on your face. Unclench your fists and stomach.

FLIGHT: Slow your roll. Ground yourself through your senses, noticing what you see, hear, smell, and taste. Take a beat before you act.

FREEZE: Move whatever you can. Wiggle your fingers or toes, breathe, shake your body out, and reconnect with yourself. Watch athletes before they perform; they shake and loosen up to avoid the freeze response.

FAWN: Claim your boundaries. Pause before saying "yes," take a few breaths, and remind yourself, "I'm safe." If you can't feel safe saying, "No," get help and get out.

FAINT: Return gently in tiny steps, using soft light, quiet comfort, or connection with a trusted person. This is an extreme response, and you should seek a doctor or therapist's help if stress is causing you to faint or sleep for long periods.

These practices prepare the body for the next step: Activating the parasympathetic system's biggest weapon: the vagus nerve.

The Vagus Nerve: Your Calm Switch

The vagus nerve is one of the longest and most important nerves in your body, stretching from your brainstem (at the back of your head, top of your neck) down through the side of your face, and through your heart, lungs, and gut. The word *vagus* means "wandering" in Latin, and that's what it does. It wanders through your organs, constantly checking in and carrying messages back to the brain about how you're doing. You could say when you get a "gut feeling," that's your vagus nerve talking. Your body is sending you a message.

Think of it as the network between mind and body. When the vagus nerve is active and strong, it tells your brain, "We're safe now. We can relax." This shifts your body out of sympathetic (fight-or-flight) mode and into parasympathetic (the paramedics bringing in rest-and-digest) mode. Your heart rate slows, your breathing deepens, and your digestion starts up again. Blood flows back to your organs instead of super-powering your muscles.

In essence, your vagus nerve is the off switch for your body's alarm system, and, like a muscle, you can strengthen it with practice. Every time you intentionally activate it, you're training your nervous system to recover faster after stress. This means shorter anxiety spirals, quicker emotional recovery, and better control over how you're feeling.

Here are a few simple ways to strengthen and activate your vagus nerve:

Slow breathing: Inhale for 6 counts, hold, exhale for 10. Longer exhales stimulate vagal tone and slow your heart rate. This is the breathing I showed you at the beginning of the book.

Cold or warm sensations: Splash cold water on your face or hold a warm compress to your neck or shoulders. Temperature shifts activate nerve endings that signal safety and getting back to balance.

Humming, singing, or chanting: The vagus nerve passes near your vocal cords, and the vibration stimulates them naturally while encouraging you to breathe rhythmically.

Movement and stretching: Running, walking, dancing, and playing sports all help release built-up stress hormones and restore your body's rhythm.

As you practice these techniques, you're not just calming yourself in the moment; you're actually retraining your biology. A strong vagus nerve "tone" means your body can shift out of fear more quickly and return to balance more easily.

This is what feeling good feels like. It's not the absence of stress, but the ability to return to calm again and again, until calm becomes your baseline. That's resilience.

Getting “The Tattoo”

I call this the Tattoo because when we designed this at the nonprofit, Bounce Back Generation, I said, "I should make this a tattoo for my wrist to remind me how to calm down."

You can think of the Tattoo Method as a vagus nerve training plan. It's a simple, repeatable process that helps your body move from stress to calm. Each step works directly with your biology to complete the stress cycle and reset your nervous system's balance. The more you do it, the stronger it gets and the faster your body learns to shift out of fear and back into safety.

Over time, the Tattoo will become your built-in reminder that you can breathe, move, speak kindly to yourself, and quiet your system.

How the Tattoo Method Works

1. Breathe: Slow breaths tell your body you're safe and help your heart slow down. You want to do a breath in for about 6 beats, hold for a sec, and out for 10. Do more than once if needed.

2. Move: Stretching or "shaking it out" helps your body release stress and leftover tension. Or do what works for you: walking, jogging, dancing, a yoga pose, punching a pillow, jumping up and down. If you're not in a place you can move, do the Full Body Squeeze (see below). Do *something* to (safely) release energy.

3. Speak Kindly: Saying kind words calms your brain and helps you feel stronger and safer. Have a phrase you can pull out of your back pocket whenever you need a pick-me-up, like "I got this," or a lyric you can sing to yourself, or lines from a poem. Something that makes you feel good. Make it your own!

4. Quiet: Taking a moment to rest lets your whole system re-

set and settle down. You don't need to do a full-on meditation session, but, if possible, take a few moments for yourself to rest, close your eyes, breathe, and clear your mind.

One thing that really helps me during Step 4, is a visualization. I imagine I'm looking at a meter where the needle is moving from the red stressed-out zone, down through the getting calm yellow zone, into the relaxed, peaceful green zone. You can imagine whatever helps you feel relaxed: maybe it's an image of a roomful of puppies, or a memory of a relaxing snooze in the sun, or a beautiful nature scene. Carry a picture around with you if it helps you visualize.

The Full Body Squeeze

Use this technique to release pent-up nervous system energy.

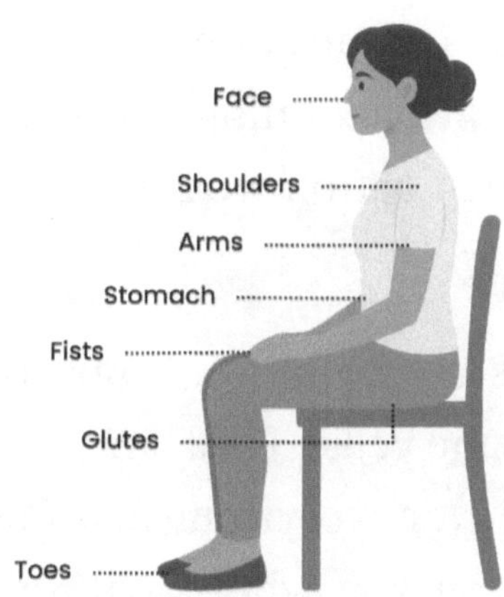

Breathe in while squeezing as many muscles as you can.

Most of the muscles you can squeeze won't be seen by anyone. It will just look like you're getting ready to take a long stretch (unless you squeeze your face, which will probably be noticeable!). Be careful not to lock your muscles and give yourself a charley horse. Hold for 5-10 seconds and release, with a soft, long exhale.

It feels great, and you can do it at work, in class, in the movie theater, on an airplane – anywhere you're feeling triggered and need to chill out.

The Charismatic Pause, or Getting Into Your Thinking Brain

You know the scene: The missile is headed toward the city, cars are crashing, people are running, sirens are blaring, and the superhero does what?

They land on a building, stand surveying the scene, and are silent, standing stoically for just a moment before leaping into action. That's something I call "The Charismatic Pause." It's like they are scanning the scene and deciding what to do next, which action would be the most effective. Their brain is working.

That's an amazing state to be in. Some people have that automatically. Someone yells, "Fire!" and people run in panic, screaming, stepping over everything in a mad rush to escape. Often, there is one person who is calm and says to their friends, "See that back door, let's go that way." They thought their way through.

Most of us have parts of our brains that shut down when we are in an intense fight or flight moment. This is normal. You're not going to sit down and calculate the wind direction and velocity of the incoming fastball to your face; you're just going to get out of the way.

Next time you are in a highly stressful situation, especially one where you're about to hit, run, scream in panic, or if you're feeling frozen, allow yourself a moment. Take a beat. Do the Charismatic Pause. Scan the situation and scan yourself. It's a moment that can change everything about how you respond. It might lead you to the way out of the situation through a side exit, instead of acting out of panicky nerves.

Here's something I have noticed: When we think someone is "cool," they tend to be people who do the Charismatic Pause. They take a beat longer to respond, and that beat allows them to calculate a response that is empowering, rather than just going off with a highly charged emotional reaction. See if you notice this too.

How We Help Each Other Stay Calm

One more calming trick to keep in mind is something you probably do automatically and are just not aware of its power.

Imagine you're at a restaurant. Suddenly, an angry diner gets up and crashes their wine glass to the floor. They yell that there is a cockroach in their soup. They're angrily gesturing, pointing to their soup bowl. Everyone's fear center in their brain is lighting up. People are murmuring. Some are grabbing their children and looking toward the exits. The manager comes out while the customer continues to yell. The manager stays calm and escorts the customer out. The whole restaurant is still uncomfortable, quietly unsure of how to react. Your waiter comes over and looks you in the eye, waves his hand, and says, "Don't worry. We know that customer. Unfortunately, they have these episodes sometimes. Everything is fine."

You and the rest of your table visibly relax. You look at each other to see how each is feeling. You return each other's glances and give each other a smile or a laugh, maybe a quick hand tap or squeeze, and get back to eating.

What just happened is something called *co-regulation*. The waiter's assurances, looking into your companion's eyes, smiling, a bit of light laughter, touching the hand of your friend next to you — all supported each other in calming down.

We can do the opposite, too. We can all dysregulate together.

Imagine a classroom on an ordinary afternoon. Everyone is talking, settling into their seats, passing papers around. Then a bee zips in through an open window. One student screams and jumps up from their desk.

Instantly, the whole room erupts. Some students leap out

of their chairs. Others freeze. A few run for the door or start looking frantically for the Raid. No one is thinking – only reacting. Notice their fight or flight freak-outs?

The bee didn't sting anyone. It didn't have to. The scream was enough to flip the whole room's nervous system into threat mode.

We have enormous power to get co-regulated in any situation, and to help others co-regulate with us.

If you just went through something terrible, look to someone who is calm and caring; they will help you regulate your reactions. Firefighters, nurses, flight attendants, and even police officers are trained to be matter-of-fact in the middle of a crisis just to help others feel OK.

Mr. Rogers used to say, "When in trouble, look for the helpers." Sometimes you need a helper, and sometimes you are the helper.

Story: *Theresa's Triumph Over Chaos*

Theresa's life started rocky. Her mother used drugs during pregnancy, and because of unsafe circumstances, she was placed in foster care right after birth. For the first few years of her life, she moved constantly. She was in a new foster home every few months. There were no steady caregivers and no reliable comfort. Doctors diagnosed her with *failure to thrive.*

When Theresa was adopted at 3 years old by a loving couple, she blossomed. But her nervous system carried scars. She had explosive tantrums. Small frustrations turned to rage. Her brain had learned that chaos and uncertainty were normal. As she got older, and over time with therapy and practice, she retrained her system to recognize safety. It wasn't easy, but Theresa knew getting calm was going to help her reach her goals. Today, in her early 20s, she's thriving.

Even when your alarm wiring is set early, healing and resilience are possible. We have neuroplasticity.

Every time you return to calm, you're proving something powerful: You are not your fear. Your body may sound the alarm, but you decide when it's time to turn it off. We will discuss more about how to feel safe again (or for the first time) in the chapters on *The Building Blocks of Protection* and *Relationships*.

WHAT IF YOU CAN'T STOP MOVING, FEELING, OR THINKING?

I have a problem. When something happens (usually work or relationship-related) where I feel put on the spot to argue, defend myself, or present an idea, my mind can get stuck in a loop. I replay the situation. I anticipate push-back. I rehearse what I'll say back, and then stop and rehearse again. I get worked up and emotional in that state, and the loop keeps going.

It's my "rumination loop," and it is annoying. Alongside my

nonprofit work, I'm also an attorney, where the job is literally to state and defend my client's position. So thinking through arguments is part of my profession.

Still, there are times when it makes me feel a little crazy when I can't turn my mind off.

Here's what's actually happening.

As we learned earlier, our nervous system evolved to respond to threats by mobilizing us to act. Stress is designed to be short-lived and physical: Something happens, the body gears up, and then the danger passes. But we often experience stress that doesn't have an immediate resolution. There's a case that needs to be argued, or a situation that needs to be confronted, or a notification of something I'm anticipating (news about funding for the year, or answering the call about a medical condition, for example) — all somewhere in the future. When that happens, the stress response doesn't simply turn off.

If your nervous system is activated into fight-or-flight, that energy has to go somewhere. If you can't fight and you can't run, your body can stay mobilized. Your emotions get hooked into that unfinished urge to act. And your mind often steps in to help by thinking, planning, rehearsing, and trying to solve the problem ahead of time.

This is why you may feel stuck in your feelings or trapped in your thoughts. Thinking becomes a stand-in for action. Rumination becomes a way to stay prepared when a resolution to the problem isn't immediately going to happen.

The tools in this chapter can help shift your state. But for me, the single most helpful first step is simply noticing: *Oh, I'm doing that overthinking thing again.* Naming it lowers the urgency. It reminds me that my brain is trying to protect me.

Even though my ruminations feel like protection because they're preparation for the future, it's totally backfiring because I get stressed, I get obsessive to the point of distraction - not to mention what the lack of sleep does to me the next day.

Here's a scenario that works for me. See if this works when your worry is keeping you up at 2 a.m.

First: I regulate my body. I do one of the practices from this chapter, The Tattoo, the Full Body Squeeze (this is especially helpful at night when I don't want to get up out of bed), or slow breathing with a long exhale. I stop trying to "solve" anything except focusing on bringing my body into a more relaxed state.

Next: I rehearse calmly. Instead of running mental simulations like *What if they misunderstand me? What if I'm not respected? What if I freeze?* I picture myself being calm, strong, and steady. I think, "I'll be able to absorb whatever comes and allow it to wash over me." The message to my emotional brain is simple: *No matter what happens, I will handle it.*

Finally, I give my mind an endpoint. I visualize putting the problem into a box. I make the box sturdy, and I put the situation "respectfully" into the box. I treat it respectfully because it is something that is meaningful to me, or I wouldn't be up at 2 a.m. running different risk analyses and scenarios, ruminating and worrying. I place it somewhere safe. A tesseract. A jeweled box. A lockbox with a velvet lining. Then I close the lid.

I tell myself: *This is important. Tomorrow is the time for it. Right now is the time for sleep.*

One last note: some of us are more prone to rumination and "stuck loops" than others. Temperament and family traits can play a role, and stress can amplify them.

If your thoughts start feeling intrusive or compulsive, or they interfere with your work, relationships, or sleep for long periods, it's a good idea to check in with a doctor or therapist. Sometimes, nervous system tools are the beginning, and sometimes you also need additional help.

The main thing for me was realizing that excessive worry is something that runs in my family. A worry gene, perhaps. That just means I'm expressing my genetics and family traits, and I'll need to find ways to manage them (a **5 Factor**).

It probably has some good sides to it, too, which have helped me to be careful and conscientious about learning, studying, and the work that I do.

Genetic traits can be a double-edged sword.

You know what can stop you from gaining mastery over your nervous system? If you believe you can't. That's why tackling your beliefs is going to be the next step in how to bounce back.

No one but you has power over your beliefs.

How are you using that power?

4
Changing Your Belief Loops

You are what you believe yourself to be. — Paulo Coelho

What do you believe about yourself?

In this chapter, you are going to learn how to recognize beliefs you hold. Then you're going to reshape them so they aren't holding you back.

There is massive power in your beliefs. Yet, for many of us, beliefs tend to be more negative than positive.

There's a theory in neuroscience called the *Bayesian Brain Hypothesis* that helps explain why our brains get stuck in negative thought patterns. Our brain constantly runs predictions based on what it already believes. It's always asking: *Given what I've seen happen before, what's the most likely thing about to happen now?*

You see, we aren't just stuck as former ape-like creatures carrying a 1.0 nervous system, dealing with a 5.0 world. Evolution has given us many tools to deal with fear, and one of those tools is our imagination.

A belief is imagining something and then looking for evidence that it is true. If your childhood environment wasn't safe, your brain learned to predict danger and developed behaviors to try to keep you safe. As you get older, your imagination may go into overdrive and imagine you're unsafe. People are talking about you behind your back, or no relationship is worth trusting – even though it's now years down the line from your childhood and you're dealing with new people and new situations.

If you believe you deserve to be safe now that you've grown, your brain can imagine what that might look like and will seek out evidence that it's true. We are constantly testing our beliefs, whether they come from fear that things will get worse or from faith that they'll get better. Beliefs can be a loop that traps us into thinking things won't change. Or they can be the engine that keeps us going when things feel impossible.

RECREATING OUR FEARFUL EXPERIENCES

Psychologists have found that we sometimes unconsciously

recreate painful situations from our past.

You might find yourself in an abusive relationship (*He's just like my father*) or put yourself in unsafe environments (*I knew the gang was trouble*).

Why do we do this? Trauma researchers suggest we're trying to master what hurt us so we can understand it, get another chance to finally "get it right," or prove we can survive it. It's called *trauma reenactment*, and it's not conscious. Our brain is trying to resolve old pain by recreating it.

Both patterns, Bayesian prediction and trauma reenactment, can keep us stuck repeating the past. But the good news is, if your brain learned these patterns, it can learn new ones. Remember, we have *neuroplasticity*. Every time you act on a new, empowering belief, you're strengthening those pathways.

CHANGING BELIEFS AND CHANGING ACTIONS

You *can* imagine something new for yourself. But it's a process.

One outcome for children who grew up with Adverse Childhood Experiences, or ACEs, is hypervigilance. They may grow up always waiting for "what's next." It's survival to keep your guard up when things have come out of the blue in the past and caught you when you were vulnerable and unprepared. You don't want that to happen ever again, which is completely understandable.

A new belief that "I'm safe now from the past" doesn't mean you have proof that you'll be safe, not yet anyway. You'll be shifting your belief even when everything around you doesn't support it being true.

If you're nervous about relying on a new belief, start slowly with a small belief. Maybe *I'm safe now*, starts like *I'm safe when I'm at home*. Then, expand it out, *I feel safe at work*, to *I'm safe in this relationship*. Continue to build from there.

That's how you start, by creating a bump, then a hill, then a mountain of new beliefs.

But the work isn't done yet. At each step, your brain will have an opportunity to seek information to support your belief, and you will need to take action, too. We will talk about how to do that, but for now, it's about daring to set up a new belief as a goal.

Let's try this. Here are some beliefs to consider. Notice your immediate reaction (positive or negative) to these statements:

I am extremely lovable, always have been, always will be.

I deserve to have my wildest dreams come true.

I have the power to feel good whenever I want.

If you responded with *Yeah, right* (eye roll), or *Yes, I do feel that inside!*, note those responses.

Some belief systems may feel unsafe to us. If I believe, "I'm lovable," and then my partner leaves me, does that mean I was fooling myself about anyone *ever* loving me?

As you now know, your nervous system tries to keep you safe, so a new positive belief may trigger a scared response. You may not want to "tempt fate" by opening up to a new relationship or "fool myself with positive thinking." It's normal to have this reaction and want to be "more realistic" with your beliefs. Just think about it like this: what are some new beliefs you might like to try on and test?

BELIEFS AS A LENS ON YOUR LIFE

Beliefs are a lens to view your life, like putting on a new pair of glasses. If you deeply believe you're unlovable and a failure, your brain will filter the world for evidence to reinforce it. If you begin to believe you're worthy of love and success, your brain starts noticing moments that reinforce that it's true.

Changing a belief is less about forcing yourself to think differently and more about showing your brain new, consistent evidence that the belief is true for you (the Bayesian theory).

Here's how belief change works:

You identify a negative belief.

You consciously adopt a new positive belief.

You take action based on that new belief.

As you act, you notice evidence through the "filter" of your new belief.

Over time, your new belief becomes a confirmed, observable fact.

Here's an example of what happens when someone isn't aware of their beliefs, and how things can change:

Story: *Paula's Distorted Vision*

Paula was treated poorly by her mother growing up. She was much younger than her older sisters, suggesting she was unexpected. Her mother often told her, "I thought I was done having kids and I could start living my life again. Then you came along." That's emotional abuse, an Adverse Childhood Experience.

Paula grew up with a warped view of her worth. She wanted to be close but also pushed people away, always seeking ways to take the upper hand so she couldn't be rejected. When things didn't go as she wanted, she saw it as a sign that she would always be the victim of uncaring people. She didn't realize it, but she didn't believe she was worthy of having good relationships.

Through her distorted lens, any time her kids or husband had a different perspective than she did, or weren't attentive enough, it signaled to her that they were rejecting her. Paula's unconscious belief, *I'm not worthy of good loving rela-*

tionships, acted as a filter. Every interaction got interpreted through that lens. A differing opinion became a rejection. A request for space became abandonment. Her husband's bad day became evidence that he didn't care about her. The belief shaped what she saw, which reinforced the belief, creating a self-perpetuating cycle.

What Paula didn't know was that she could take off those lenses and try on another pair that suggested: *I am lovable. People are not rejecting me. My mother's words were wrong.*

Her daughter said to her one day, "Mom, you push everyone away and then blame us for leaving."

Perhaps she heard her daughter, or the pain became too uncomfortable, but eventually Paula started therapy and began practicing her new belief: *I am worthy of good relationships. When people disagree with me, they're not rejecting me.* It didn't happen overnight.

One day, she noticed that her children didn't call as often as her friend's kids did. It felt awful, and she thought: Does this mean they don't care about me? She looked instead for evidence that they do. They sent her money for support, they brought their children over at least once a month, and they were thoughtful about giving her gifts she said she wanted. That was evidence that she had a good relationship with them.

It was a difficult transition. Paula had to learn to interpret the data she was getting from her family differently than she was used to.

ARE YOU LIVING FROM BELIEFS OR LIVING FROM CIRCUMSTANCES?

Here's a way to look at how beliefs affect our circumstances. We can look at how we form our experiences by seeing our mental process like concentric circles, or like a target.

This model will help you understand whether you're living outward from your beliefs, or letting circumstances crash inward to form what you believe.

1. Living from Beliefs (Living from the Inside Out)

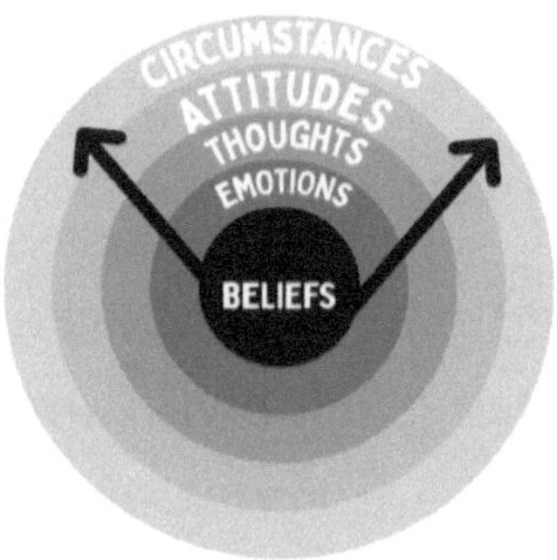

When you live from your center, your core belief radiates outward through each layer of your life: Your belief shapes your emotions, which inform your thoughts, which create your actions, which result in your circumstances.

2. Living from your Circumstances (Living from the Outside

In)

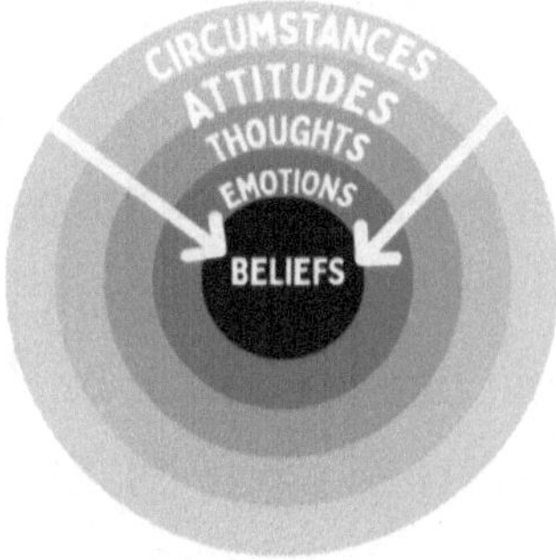

Many of us live reactively. External circumstances are what form our beliefs. We interpret what they mean, and then they work their way inward, layer by layer, until they form a core belief: Circumstances (overdue bills, bad relationships, work losses) drive our actions (panicking, numbing or reacting with anger), which color our thoughts (*Life is against me*), which spiral into emotions (despair, anxiety, stress), until a belief sets in at our core: *Things just don't work out for me*, or *life is stressful, that's just how it is.*

Story: *George and Laura's Different Lenses*

George grew up in an unstable environment when it came to money. There were many ups and downs. Sometimes, it was luxury travel and expensive schools; at others, the light bill didn't get paid, and the household was in cold darkness. George's father always worried about money. When he worked, things were great. But work life was unstable for George's dad, and when he lost his job, they would be plunged into near bankruptcy.

Eventually, things would pick up again. It was a constant cycle.

Today, George has a great job, as does his wife, and they are financially stable. But George's belief that disaster is just around the corner, just like it was for his father, keeps him up at night thinking about the "what ifs." It drives his wife crazy because he tosses and turns, keeping her up too.

George's wife, Laura, grew up on a farm where there were good years and bad years. She believed that during good years, they celebrated, but also saved. When bad years came around, they felt good knowing they could make things instead of buying, grow their own food, and entertain themselves with crafts and hobbies.

George catastrophized even while living very comfortably, and Laura stayed calm, knowing she could enjoy life regardless of their income level.

One day, the worst thing that could happen happened. Like his father, George lost his job.

Let's just stop for a moment and consider how the 5 Factors would affect George. His nervous system is more easily triggered by childhood experiences, there are current environmental aspects, and he had generational trauma. Those all added more stress to the meaning of the event.

OK, let's continue our story.

Here's how George's "circumstances-reactive" pattern formed (working from outside in):

George: Circumstance: I *lost my job. It's happening, just like my dad!* Action: Stays up at night worrying. Attitude: *This always happens, just when things are going well, everything falls apart.* Thought: I *need to worry about everything and anticipate the worst possible scenarios.* Emotion: high anxiety. Belief (formed at core): I *will never have a stable financial life. I'm cursed.*

Here's how Laura's "belief-centered" pattern works (from inside out):

Laura: Belief (at core): I *am resourceful and capable of handling my finances regardless of my situation.* Emotion: Calm determination. Thought: *Money comes and goes, but I can handle it either way.* Attitude: I *always find creative solutions to get through lean times.* Action: Makes a budget, saves, looks for ways to increase income, and finds inexpensive activities to do. Circumstance: Occasional money challenges don't freak her out, and she can problem-solve without panic.

Does believing something actually change what happens? Or does it just change how you feel about what happens?

The answer is both! Your beliefs don't magically change external circumstances. Laura can't control George's work. She can say, "I can't believe they laid you off!" but you know:

Believe it. It's reality.

However, beliefs absolutely can change your responses to circumstances. Laura's belief that she's resourceful means she creates budgets, finds solutions, and doesn't panic. Those actions create different outcomes than George's anxiety-driven responses. He might get depressed for a few weeks, feel dejected, and doubt himself. That might delay his job search, or have him showing up to interviews lacking energy, or exuding anxiety.

Beliefs drive actions, and actions create results. There *is* some magical stuff about beliefs we will explore later, but for now, just know that beliefs do hold power over your circumstances.

HOW TO UNCOVER YOUR BELIEFS

A lot of us don't consciously know what we believe. Our beliefs operate in the background, quietly shaping or distorting how we experience life.

You can't change what you don't know.

Here are two ways to bring your beliefs into your awareness:

Method 1: Meditative Practice

Meditation helps you clear away the noise so you can hear what's underneath. When you meditate, you learn to quiet the many voices in your mind and access a deeper sense of communication with yourself and (if you believe in it) with something larger than yourself, like your higher consciousness, God, the universe; you decide.

In meditation, you can ask yourself: *What do I believe about ____?*

Now keep digging. Just like you might ask a friend, "How are you feeling about this?" and they say, "Fine," and you say, "No, how are you really feeling?" You need to ask yourself, *Is this what I really believe? Or is there something underneath?*

If you would like to do a meditation on uncovering your beliefs, you'll find a link to the Bounce Back Generation YouTube Channel for a guided meditation. See the resources page at the end of the book.

Method 2: "What's Really Going On?" Method

If meditation isn't your thing, the second way to uncover beliefs is to pay attention in the moment when something doesn't go your way.

Ask yourself: *What do I believe about this situation?*

This is an ongoing conversation you'll have with yourself over your lifetime, constantly testing your belief system.

When you uncover what you think you believe, ask again: *Is there another, underlying belief I have about this?*

You can use this technique whether things go well or not. When something exciting and positive happens, ask: *What do I believe about this situation?* You may be surprised to find that even though you're having a positive experience, you have secret negative beliefs about what it means or how it will end.

Let's see how this might work.

Story: *Denise's Sabotaging Beliefs*

Denise is a smart woman. She believes she can handle just about anything, and she usually does. But when it comes to work, people notice she always finds a way to sabotage herself. When the job is going well, she starts looking for what's wrong with her workplace, her supervisor, or her colleagues.

Her friends can see it coming. She'll be at a job for six months and think it's great. By month seven, she'll say her supervisor isn't as smart as she initially thought. She'll second-guess workplace rules and start gossiping about coworkers' bad habits. Eventually, she can't hide her growing dissatisfaction. She either quits in frustration or gets let go.

Denise's underlying belief is that she would be a better boss than virtually every other boss she's ever had. She may be right. But she's unaware of her belief that *she* should be the boss.

If she asked herself, *What do I really believe about myself in my career?* She might recognize that the role that aligns with her is as the queen bee, not a worker drone. With this awareness, she could start applying for supervisor positions instead of signing up for the wrong roles.

But consider this: What if Denise realized she believes she's meant to be a leader in the workplace? Would she be able to align her emotions behind that belief? She also might believe she doesn't have the right degree, or that, as a woman in her industry, she won't be taken seriously.

We can have unconscious and conflicting beliefs. Without this awareness, Denise will likely repeat this pattern for years, wondering why every job goes bad sooner or later.

Questions to Ask Yourself Regularly

Get in the habit of asking yourself these questions. Write them down. Journal about them. Come back to them over time and notice how your answers shift. You might be surprised at what surfaces.

What do I believe about my personality?

What do I believe about my worth as a person?

What do I believe my past says about me that I cannot change?

What do I believe about my future?

What do I believe I'm capable of?

Your answers will reveal patterns. Maybe you believe you're capable in some areas but not others. Maybe you trace everything back to that one big experience that happened when you were little. That's valuable information. These beliefs have been running in the background, and now you can bring them into the light.

Building New Beliefs: A Practice

Once you've identified a limiting belief, here's how to begin changing it:

Step 1: Write down the old belief. Example: "I'm not worthy of having a good relationship."

Step 2: Ask yourself: Where did this belief come from?

Example: "My father left when I was young. My mother was always critical. I learned early that I had to earn love through achievement."

Step 3: Ask yourself: Is this belief serving me?

Example: "No. It keeps me isolated and prevents me from forming deep connections. I'm exhausted from trying to earn what should be freely given."

Step 4: Use your imagination: What would I rather believe?

Example: "I am worthy of love just by existing. My past doesn't determine my worth."

Step 5: Ask: What evidence supports this new belief?

Example: "My friend has always shown up for me when I

needed her. My dog loves me unconditionally. I've survived hard things, which shows I'm resilient and valuable. I know children deserve to be loved just for being. Why should I be different?"

Step 6: Act as if the new belief is true. This is the hardest part. You may not fully believe it at first. That's totally OK. Start taking small actions that line up with the new belief, whatever it is. Reach out to that new potential friend. Write that poem. Take a lesson. Try out for the team. Form a band. Take the trip. Each action reinforces a new pathway in your brain.

Step 7: Repeat, repeat, repeat. Remember neuroplasticity? You *can* change. You're literally rewiring your brain. But it can take time, so be patient with yourself!

One complicating factor we saw in Denise's story is that we often hold conflicting beliefs simultaneously. You might believe *I'm capable of great things*, AND *I'll probably fail.* Both can be true in your mind at once. When you uncover conflicting beliefs, you'll need to choose which one you want to strengthen.

WHAT BELIEF CHANGE FEELS LIKE

Changing beliefs isn't like flipping a light switch.

At first, the new belief will feel fake, like you're lying to yourself. You'll say, *I can be an A student this year*, and your old belief will shout back, *You're not smart enough! When have you ever done well at school? You're terrible at test-taking.*

That's normal. Keep going. Over weeks, you'll notice small shifts. Instead of coming home and turning on your gaming console or scrolling mindlessly for hours, you pick up your books and get homework done.

Things don't go well right away. You take a test and fail.

You say, *Failing isn't who I am anymore. I'm becoming an* A *student.* You meet with your counselor to find out about tutoring for test-taking.

Over months, the new belief starts to feel more natural. You catch yourself acting from the new belief without thinking about it. You don't miss a class. You start a study group with a couple of friends. You give yourself rewards every time you apply your new test-taking skills. You may not be manifesting the reality of your new belief yet, but it's a start. (We will talk more about when "reality" doesn't match your beliefs in the next chapter on manifesting.)

Now, let me offer a different way to look at beliefs. It's less scientific, more philosophical. It's fun, but it can also be surprisingly useful.

THE MYSTERY AND MAGIC OF BELIEFS

Is belief faith or magical? There is something mysterious at work when we decide to believe. Let's explore next what might be going on.

For some people, believing in something they can't see yet is too much to ask, especially when years go by, and failures have piled up.

Part of what you're being asked to do when you decide to believe in something is to stake a claim. That means standing on ground that may not be fully supported by evidence, but holding on to a belief anyway.

The overall message is to be the Decider. You decide what you believe and find the magical power in that while you work with reality.

Joe's Story: Reality, or Magical Belief?

Joe believed he was a great saxophone player. He spent years teaching himself, taking a few community college courses, listening to jazz, and studying YouTube videos. He believed he could make it as a professional musician. However, he was unsure where to start because paying gigs wanted professional band experience or a degree from a music college. Joe tried a few open auditions, but they didn't go anywhere.

At some point, reality intervened: He needed to make money to pay his bills. Should he follow his belief or let it go? Did he need to accept that his music was a hobby, nothing more?

Before deciding, Joe wanted to test his belief: Could he be a professional musician? Did audiences like him?

Joe decided he would play his sax in the subway. He found a good spot with a lot of traffic and set up a hat for donations.

Most people scurried by, but a few stopped to listen. He got about $7 in his hat that day.

There are two scenarios that could play out after that subway experiment.

Scenario #1: Joe could say, *That's it. I've got all the evidence I need. I can't make it as a musician. I should have had $100 in that hat and crowds cheering for me.*

Scenario #2: Joe could just as easily say, *Today went so well! I'm really inspired. I earned enough for a coffee and made some people feel good on their commute.*

Can you detect the magic?

Joe decides whether he reads the information as a sign to give up, or a sign of encouragement (or at least not defeat).

Joe not only decides what he believes is true, but he also interprets what reality is showing him. He is the "measurer" of reality. Neither interpretation of the subway performance is wrong. The question is: How much does his belief matter to him?

I know some of you skeptics might be thinking: What if Joe plays in subways for the rest of his life, waiting for his big break? Don't worry, we will talk about that kind of scenario in the next chapter.

OK, so we've talked about changing limiting beliefs to empowering ones. But there's one more belief shift that can be transformative. You'll have to bear with me through this next section.

WHAT NEAR DEATH MIGHT TELL US ABOUT LIFE?

Here's a bit of a mind-bending idea that might completely change how you see your struggles: What if you chose your circumstances before you were born? What if you created the game you're playing now, and you're the main character?

This may sound a little woo-woo or even like I'm being thoughtless, especially if you've been through harsh experiences. I don't want to say that what you've gone through isn't awful, unfair, or painful.

Still. Stay with me for a moment, because whether this is literally true doesn't matter as much as what happens when you believe it might be.

Over the past few decades, researchers have documented thousands of near-death experiences (NDEs): people who died clinically and were revived. Their stories share many amazing similarities across cultures, religions, and backgrounds. They describe floating above their bodies, moving through darkness toward a bright light, meeting deceased loved ones or beings of light, and feeling an overwhelming sense of peace, love, and belonging.

Many say they felt more "at home" in that place than they ever felt on Earth. Even years later, some say they long to return but realize they have things they want to do here.

A significant number of people who've had NDEs report that during their experience, they understood their life on Earth was something they designed. They chose their circumstances, their challenges, even their family, sometimes with the guidance of wiser beings or their own higher consciousness.

They chose these specific difficulties to learn lessons, develop certain skills, and experience emotions that aren't possible in the peaceful realm they visited.

Similar themes emerge from past life regression studies. That's where people under hypnosis or deep meditation describe memories of previous lives and what they say they experienced *in between lives*. Researchers like Dr. Brian Weiss, former Head of Psychiatry at Mount Sinai Medical Center in Miami and author of several books on his findings on past life regressions, and Dr. Michael Newton, a therapist and author of the book *Journey of the Souls*, have documented thousands of cases where people describe planning their life circumstances before birth. They say they chose their parents, arranged their major challenges, and even made plans to meet up with certain people along the way.

I'm not asking you to believe this is literally true. Maybe it is. Maybe it's not. Maybe it's the brain creating meaning during hypnosis or when deprived of oxygen. What I do know is that this perspective can be incredibly empowering for some.

Think about it. If you believe you're a victim of random bad luck, you were born into the wrong family, dealt a terrible hand, cursed by fate ... that belief creates helplessness.

It's basically looking at your **5 Factors** and seeing them as either a curse, a challenge, or a gift - or even all three.

What if some part of you, your soul, your higher self, your consciousness, chose this life, knowing it would be hard, because you wanted to develop specific strengths? What if your worst experiences are actually the training ground for your greatest strengths?

That sounds a lot like a Hero's Journey to me.

This belief doesn't erase the pain. It doesn't make abuse OK or trauma justified. I don't think you deserve the bad things that happened to you.

Instead, what I like about this idea is that you can explore shifting your perception of yourself from

Why am I so unlucky?

to

What am I learning from this? What superpower am I building?

Think of it like you're playing some crazy cosmic video game.

This "So-Called Life" Video Game

Try to imagine: What if your life were like a video game where you selected the quest, set up the characters, and invented challenges. Could you tell a story about your life that was like a game?

If you designed a video game, you're more than the player. You're the genius developer who came up with the storyline, created characters, plots, and levels, and now you're playing and honing your skills through trial and error and failures, to finally win the game. As the game developer, what "winning" means is also up to you.

Your life isn't a game, but thinking about it this way can help shift how you see things.

Struggles gain meaning. They're not random suffering. They're part of a curriculum you designed. The harder the class, the more you're learning. The more you know, the more personal power you have.

If you chose this (on some level), then fighting reality is fighting your own wisdom or deeper need to experience something powerful (good and bad).

Part of the Near Death Experiences and past life lore is that in your afterlife, like a video game, you realize you don't really die. When you play a video game and you "die", your player falls to the ground, gets Xs on its eyes, and it's game over. For now.

You, the real you, gets up, stretches, and makes some lunch.

You don't have to believe this concept to play around with it!

IT'S NOT YOUR FAULT, BUT YOU STILL HAVE TO DEAL WITH REALITY

As I talked about in *Chapter 1*, many things have shaped who you are today. There are events you cannot change: ingrained biological/nervous system responses, DNA, family histories, and the messy, intense, and often unfair world we live in.

Having beliefs that defeat us is a way to protect ourselves from hoping against hope that things will change. *I'll never make it* is another way of saying, *I need to protect myself at all costs from everything, including being deeply disappointed.* Totally understandable.

Reality will throw obstacles at you like a villain in a superhero movie. You will experience setbacks, rejections, cruelty, and bad characters blocking your way.

As heroes, we have had to keep climbing anyway. And it is hard, no doubt about it.

Having beliefs that are protective is smart. But they may be limiting us from reaching for our heroic future. If you are going to live a heroic life, you have to start with the courage to believe in something different while you are also grappling with the reality of "how things are."

Psychology tells us our beliefs are shaped not just by internal logic but by interacting with others and with the world around us. People and reality give us information and feedback all the time, whether we like it or not. That means we have to work with reality, not against it.

A hero must be able to set and attain their goals. Some people call this "manifesting." It's the key that takes us from sitting on the couch wishing life were different, to standing on the mountaintop of your accomplishments with your cape waving in the wind behind you. Let's find out how manifestation works.

5

Is Quantum Manifestation Real?

We are part of this universe; we are in this universe, but more important than these facts, the universe is in us. – Neil deGrasse Tyson

We've all tried to will something into existence. Sometimes it works. Sometimes it feels like we're screaming into the void. Nothing happens. So how do we actually turn our beliefs and desires into something real?

You've probably heard people talk about *manifesting*, the idea that your thoughts or vibrations can shape the universe so you get what you want. Some of you might remember the book *The Secret*, which was also made into a popular movie. *The Secret* said, in a nutshell, that if you can imagine it, you can attract it.

Today, *The Secret* has been blended with quantum theory and taken on a new life and new popularity. The basic idea is that our consciousness can literally move subatomic particles into becoming the things we want.

MANIFESTATION: THE REAL V. THE REEL

Let's dive into the science a little.

Quantum physics describes a world where tiny particles behave differently when they are observed or measured. The basics of quantum physics are that a particle (the stuff that is smaller than an atom) is both a particle and a wave, but you don't know what it is going to be until you take a look and measure it. Until then, the stuff everything is made of is just a *probability* of what could be. Meaning anything you want is nothing yet — until you will it into being something you want. That's at least the popular version of quantum manifestation.

This idea will be familiar to you if you watched the Marvel Avengers movie series.

The superheroes in the Avengers universe not only battle the bad guys, but they also have to do so interdimensionally, where different universes have different outcomes. This means there are multiple possibilities of events happening in multiple universes.

It's a cool idea to pick the timeline you want to be in and surf over to the life you want.

The manifestation movement claims that if you can adjust your vibration to the life you want, you will embody it. The new idea isn't just that you should imagine what you want. It's also that you should vibrate in alignment with what you want. It's more "be it to have it."

By focusing your energy on what you want, visualizing, and holding yourself in the energy of having it, you're somehow influencing reality at the quantum level into manifesting your desired outcome. Perhaps it means seeking new timelines where you're living the dream you want.

It's tempting to think that by just wanting something badly enough, our consciousness can reshape the world.

Many people have tried to think or "vibrate" their way into success, but I've never met anyone who has used this process and consistently gotten results. I do know that it requires a lot of positive thinking, which can feel like mental gymnastics. "Don't think bad thoughts" is really hard if you don't see results.

Let's consider a few things: Is it possible to reorder reality by focusing our minds and aligning our beliefs? Can we timeline jump? And if we can, should we?

What if you jump to a world where you are a successful entrepreneur, but in this new timeline, your marriage is awful, and your beloved dog is now a cat? As the manifestation movement claims, can we adjust our vibration so it connects with the life we dream of?

While I find these ideas intriguing, for me, they're not realistic. Let me share with you how I understand quantum physics *really* works to help us manifest the life we want.

Don't worry, I'm not going to tell you there isn't something happening at a quantum level. I'm just going to adjust what is really going on based on quantum science as we know it today.

GETTING THE UNIVERSE TO SUPPORT YOUR DREAMS

Here's a different way to look at the idea of manifestation using quantum theory that I think is more exciting and, in my experience, has far more evidence of success than simply focusing on what you want and waiting for reality to respond.

I am not a physicist, but if you were to ask a physicist how they manifest their desires into reality, they would say they're trying to make their life work, just like the rest of us.

Most will say this about the pop culture quantum manifestation theories: "That's not how any of this works."

Most popular quantum manifestation theories online are not based on science, and in my experience, just make people feel disappointed.

Perhaps your experience is different, but I'm about sharing practical information that I know works in most cases. I don't want anyone to finish this book feeling frustrated.

Having said that, you won't be disappointed by the more scientifically based idea of quantum manifestation. What is actually borne out by the science, and the opinions of *actual* quantum physicists, is profoundly more fascinating and useful.

Quantum Physics 101

Quantum physics tells us that, deep down, everything in the universe exists as possibilities. Electrons don't sit still. They hover between "maybe it's this/maybe it's that" (an oversimplification) until something interacts with them. That's the famous *observer effect* that people often use to convince themselves to set an intention and align with the frequency of that intention.

They will say that because a wave becomes a particle when observed, it means our consciousness affects its state of being. "I want X to happen" means, at a quantum level, reality reorganizes itself to fit our desires.

I wish quantum physics supported this concept of manifestation. I want to be able to say a few Harry Potter-like spells and watch things line up like I want them to.

I am reminded of someone I know who told me that when she was in middle school and realized Harry Potter wasn't real, she was depressed for weeks.

But all is not lost! Let's not get depressed. Let's get informed.

In those famous quantum experiments, light (aka photons)

hits matter and forces it to "decide" where to be. Until they interact with something, they exist as a cloud of probabilities. Not *here* or *there*, but *possibly* here or there. When that interaction happens, one possibility becomes real (manifested). That's the physics.

The observer effect doesn't mean you can just think really hard about something you want and *voilà*, your wish is granted. In quantum physics, "observation" means interacting with the environment or whatever is being used to measure it, not human consciousness.

That means our thoughts don't collapse the wave function. But they can change what you notice, what you act on, and which opportunities you pursue.

You can shift probabilities by becoming a master at observing and responding to reality (i.e. what's going on around you). Probabilities still exist (and one of them is what you want), but you have to also take action.

Think of it this way: Before you commit to a goal, you're standing in a hallway with many doors. Each door represents a possible future. When you walk through one it means you're committing to the goal behind that door. Once you enter, you're in a space where new information, relationships, and feedback become available (i.e., you're working with reality).

Quantum physics says that reality becomes more *defined* through interaction. It doesn't operate only through our imagination.

Stepping through a door is the moment you move from possibility into participating with reality that's lined up with your goal.

Another term for reality would be "information coming to you from this specific set of probabilities."

Once you are through that door, reality starts showing you things, not because you're bending space/time but because you are in a relationship with the thing you desire.

Let's put it all together now:

Visualizing: The Hall of Doors

Walk down the hallway of doors. They have various labels like "Become a famous actor on Broadway" or "Be a diving coach at my swim club," or this one, which says: "Buy my dream home by the end of next year." You enter that door.

Now, you are in a field where it is possible for you to begin to align with the probabilities of the room, which is to buy a house.

When you step through a door you become engaged with what's inside and all the people, systems, opportunities, and consequences that go along with it. Engagement starts to turn a vague dream into a lived reality. You are no longer imagining a future. You are in a *relationship* with it.

Now that you're in the room for the "dream home next

year," you're going to be acting toward that goal. You are saving money, keeping track of your credit and income, researching neighborhoods, and touring homes. You're interacting within the "probability space" of "new home next year."

"Quantum manifestation" really means you are an active participant in bringing things into reality. You're constantly collecting information, and that process is both *conscious and unconscious* (more on that below).

The main point is that manifestation is not about forcing reality to bend to your conscious choices. It's about recognizing a potential outcome within a field of possibilities, and aligning your attention, choices, and actions with its "reality field."

But, you're not done yet. To make the reality you want come forth, you'll need your mind, body, and emotions involved.

YOU NEED YOUR FULL SELF IN YOUR MANIFESTATION PROCESS

Your thoughts and beliefs are extremely powerful. They coordinate with reality. That coordination also involves your nervous system lining up and being able to tune your brain to what you want. Then, you'll need to be an excellent observer and interpreter of reality.

What does that mean?

Let's start with the basics: Do you want something really badly? When you think about getting it, does your body react in fear?

Do you think: *What if I don't get it? What if I try, and it's a waste of time? What if everyone laughs at my dreams because they are impossible*? Boom. Your fear just killed your dream.

In everyday life, you are manifesting through "imagining," but you're going to have to get your brain and body to support you. *Come with me, brain and body. Let's go make this happen.*

You need to bring all of you into the process.

Neuroscience and psychology tell us that when you want something, and you're excited, happy, and hopeful, your brain and body begin to reorganize.

Here's an illustration of how it happens:

The Quantum Manifestation of a Grilled Cheese Sandwich

Think of this scenario: You're sitting on the couch, and you say, "I really want a grilled cheese sandwich." Your brain says "Yes!" and starts to think, "Do I have bread, cheese, and butter in the fridge?"

Your body gets up and pulls together the ingredients, and in a few minutes, that buttery, cheesy, warm goodness is in your mouth and heading down to your stomach. You just "manifested" a grilled cheese sandwich.

What happened? Your brain thought of the sandwich, and

with it came a little zing of dopamine. Dopamine is a neurotransmitter that also acts as a hormone, and it controls your movement, motivation, and anticipation of a reward.

Think back to our ancient grandparents in the cave. If they were hungry and just sat around waiting for food to come in and lie down for them, they were going to starve. Dopamine got them excited and energized to go out to hunt and gather.

Let's put this together with what we learned in past chapters. First, you need to know what you really want to happen.

What do you desire? This is your heroic quest. Be specific.

Next, you consider your 5 Factors, meaning you've got to consider where you're starting from. If you want to make a grilled cheese sandwich on the North Pole, for example (your Environment Factor), and you're sitting in the snow with no store around, you'll need to take that reality into account.

Now, you'll need to Tame Your Nervous System and make sure it is on board, too. If you found out you were out of cheese, your anger and frustration might cause you to give up in frustration — or compel you to walk to the corner store for the ingredients.

You need to Believe You Can Have It. You believe that grilled cheese sandwich is definitely something you can have. You deserve it!

If the ingredients are not available, you're not going to give up and say, "Well, I guess I'll starve." You're either heading to the store or finding something else to satisfy your craving. If you're at the North Pole, you're sending out signals to get a plane to come get you and take you to the nearest store.

See how things line up to make reality fit what you just imagined in your head a few minutes ago?

It's no different for any other thing your heart desires. You may want something bigger, takes more time, needs more ingredients, and you're not sure of all the steps to make it happen — but it's the same process.

WHAT'S THE QUANTUM DIFFERENCE?

Here's what quantum mechanics shows us, and to me, this is the exciting part: Everything in the universe is connected through constant interaction, at least at the quantum level.

We exist in what physicist Carlo Rovelli calls a *web of relations*. As Rovelli writes: "Everything is what it is only with respect to something else." That means other objects and interactions actually *define* what something is. Rovelli is describing relationships between quantum systems.

So, it's not that the wave or particle is out there floating in space on its own. It's part of an infinite web of interactions with other particles. Everything is waiting for something or someone to interact with it.

This is where a little philosophy can help develop the concept a little more. It's like that old Zen question: "If a tree falls in the forest and no one is there to hear it, was there a sound?" This is the mystery of the power of observation. When we pay attention to something, we change how it shows up in our world.

If you start asking yourself, *What are some ways I could make a million dollars?*, you're already influencing your personal reality because your focus shapes what you notice, what you act on, and which opportunities you take. It's the same reason that when you're thinking about buying a specific car, you suddenly start seeing it everywhere.

We're interconnected. A string pulled here tugs on a string somewhere else.

Buddhist monk Thích Nhất Hạnh teaches that everything "inter-is." In his book *Interbeing*, he describes how even a single page of his book contains the whole cosmos: the sunlight that grew the trees, the rain that fed the trees that became the paper, the people who made the pages. Even the carbon and other elements originating from distant stars were used to make the ink for the book.

The idea of being separate from anything doesn't make sense.

Why do I find this concept so exciting when it comes to manifestation? Because on both an intellectual and emotional level, we are never creating alone. The Earth, the sun, all of the constant activities happening around us, and the stuff from exploding stars billions of years ago are participating in everything we do.

We are, as Dr. Tyson says, part of the universe; it's around us, in everything we want. And it is in us too.

That means our conscious awareness and intention are part of what shapes reality. It doesn't control it, but it shapes it. Because everything impacts everything else in some distant or immediate way.

Now, here's a great belief to try on right now. This is not science or "quantum"; it's you bringing the power of your beliefs to the equation:

I believe that the elements of Earth, the stars, and reality itself want me to succeed and achieve my goals to the highest degree possible. I feel the whole of the cosmos is rooting for me.

Does that feel true, or do you feel that for anything you want, you must work super hard at it and fight forces lined up against you?

Trauma, especially in childhood, can leave you with a sense that the world is not your friend and no one is on your side.

That means before we can co-create with the universe, we have to feel safe enough to trust it.

DOES THE UNIVERSE WANT US TO HAVE WHAT WE WANT?

I would argue that our natural state is to trust that reality will support us in our dreams.

Babies are born open, expecting and needing loving care. But over time, that natural state changes when fearful things happen. We trade believing good things are possible, for trying to feel safe from harm. This is normal.

But, for our own evolution, we need to be able to consciously reset these negative, fearful states, so we can embrace that true trusting nature again. It means we need to give ourselves the time, tools, and opportunity to heal.

Then, we need to start building our authentic and active power to make our dreams come true. If you can start your Hero's Journey with even a sliver of trust that your happiness is going to be supported, that's where quantum physics can be an inspiring metaphor.

Armed with the belief that reality wants to help you win because it contains multiple (maybe infinite?) states of possibilities, your attention and awareness determine which potential reality you act upon to bring into reality.

I can see how this can get confused with "my consciousness moves quantum particles." What I'm saying is more grounded in real life experiences I've gained from working with people who are struggling with many of the **5 Factors** in their lives. They need real steps that work, and most have zero trust in anything working for them because so much has been stacked against them.

But, giving someone steps that work means showing how powerful their attention is to the things they want. When we've lived in constant chaos and uncertainty, learning to trust that dreams can come into fruition is really hard. But once we know what we want, and believe it is possible, then our focused attention becomes the magic "quantum" pixie dust that turns probabilities into reality.

A way to interpret what's happening at a quantum level is that the universe is waiting for you to notice it. Notice what is possible. Then interact with it. You're the magic in the equation because no one else but you can make your specific dreams a reality. Seeing your manifestation journey as a loving challenge, a quest that is guided by a generous hand, makes you a main player character in the gambling casino of probabilities we call reality.

Maybe a story will help to make my explanation clear.

The Quantum Casino: A Manifestation Story

Let's say you're an actual gambler, and you're going to play the odds in a Las Vegas casino. Note: *Real casinos are rigged against players. But let's imagine this is a perfect quantum casino where the universe's math rules.*

You walk into the casino with a dream: "I'm going to make a million bucks." You're certain that's what you want. You believe it's possible; others have won big here. Your belief is strong, and right now, you feel the probabilities are simply waiting for you to engage with them.

With $200 in your pocket, you approach the blackjack table and place your bet. Five minutes later, you've lost $50.

Reality just gave you information: You don't actually know how to play blackjack.

So, you adapt. You step back and watch other players, studying their strategies. After observing for a while, you notice something interesting, not about blackjack, but about how people react to the game. Their faces light up with hope. They lean in to watch the cards flip. Even when they lose, some of them giggle.

You head over to the roulette table to try your luck there. No luck. But watching that wheel spin triggers something in your mind. You notice: *Look at how excited people get during that moment of anticipation.* You think there's something almost meditative about watching it spin, not knowing where it will land. Why is that so compelling?

After losing more money at roulette, you sit down at the bar a bit discouraged. Maybe this million-dollar dream isn't meant to be. Maybe you should just go back to your regular job and forget this whole thing.

You get some lunch. Fried rice from the Chinese place. There's your fortune cookie. You open it: *Your dreams will manifest soon.* Your heart leaps a bit. Is this a sign to keep playing?

You hit the tables again. Sigh. No luck.

But something keeps nagging at you. That roulette wheel. The way people seem to love that feeling of anticipation as they watch the wheel spin: "maybe this time ..."

An idea enters your mind: *What if there was a wheel that didn't give you money, but gave you something else you need? What if it gave you encouragement? Like a fortune cookie saying?*

You grab a napkin and start sketching. A decorative wheel you could put by your front door. Every morning before you leave the house, you spin it and get a message: *Don't be fooled by yesterday's failures. You will find what you seek.* Or, *Today your dreams will materialize into reality.*

You rush home with $50 left in your pocket and start building a prototype. You call it the "You-Lett Me Feel Good Machine™" (get it? Roulette – You-lett?). Ha.

Six months later, you have a working prototype.

One year later, you're ready to start selling your contraption.

At first, nobody gets it. "Can't you just make this a phone app?" people ask. No!

You pivot again. You set up demonstrations outside grocery stores. You sell them out of your car at farmers' markets, sports events, and flea markets. You create an online store. You refine the fortune messages. You improve the design and find manufacturers. You get loans from banks and friends, and you deal with shipping problems and customer service.

Two years after walking into that casino with a dream and $200 in gambling money, you make your first million dollars in profits.

So, what happened?

A desire ("I want a million dollars") met a belief ("This is possible").

That belief gave you the courage to take action (enter the casino).

Reality responded with information (you lost money but gained by being open to the “quantum” of possibilities).

A creative insight emerged (the roulette plus fortune cookie message concept).

You took new action that lined up with that insight (built a prototype, tested the market, and refused to give up).

The universe didn't just hand you a million dollars. You co-created with reality. You noticed what was there (the roulette wheel, people's faces, the feeling of anticipation). You tried, you adapted, and you tried again. You stayed engaged with possibilities instead of giving up when the first probability (winning a million at the casino tables) didn't work out.

WHAT IF YOU DON'T BELIEVE?

I, probably like you reading this, have not had the perfect life. Things were not handed to me, and I have experienced my own share of trauma, pain, disappointments, and failures. I watch the news every day and see that we live on what I call the universe's murder/prison planet. Yes, I have a dark side.

It can be a struggle to see life differently. But it is possible to view things from a brighter angle. We can flip the light switch on when establishing our beliefs. Like in the Matrix, we can peek behind the curtain. Are we in bondage or light?

The point is, it is a choice. That doesn't mean the path is always easy. But believe me, choosing the light path takes the same amount of energy as walking a dark one. Having hope is, in itself, a superpower.

If you're struggling with depression, severe anxiety, or other mental health challenges, manifestation steps might feel impossible. That's where you know that healing needs to happen. The practical steps in this chapter will still be there when you're ready. And remember, sometimes the thing you need to manifest is getting the right kind of help. That, my friend, is a perfectly valid goal.

You may find in your healing process what I had to discover.

I had to shift from dark thoughts to the belief that everything is lovingly connected, or at least not cruelly connected.

I cannot feel like I'm constantly fighting reality when I want something. I see that we are *inter-being* with reality, dancing with it, and it wants to give us what we want. But it wants us to learn its ways and join it in the dance toward making something turn from a particle of possibility to an observable/measurable and created fact. That's the same process, whether you're quantum manifesting your dreams or using quantum physics to make a computer chip.

Quantum theory shows us that we are always co-creating with reality, not by just observing it or measuring it, but by being a part of it, weaving different strings of thoughts, actions, and information together to make something new.

This is the Bounce Back way and the Hero's path: We allow life to show us it loves us.

The Nun and the Fly

Years ago, I watched an interview that really stuck with me. A very young nun in Central America during a time of civil unrest was taken prisoner by the military for her human rights work. She told her story years later, after her release.

She had been held in solitary confinement for months. Being alone is extremely punishing for humans because belonging and being with others is a deep human need.

During those torturous months, she longed for company and one day prayed for someone to talk to. Suddenly, she noticed a fly in her cell. It buzzed around, landed on the wall, and stayed.

In her loneliness, she began to speak to the fly, to tell the fly her fears, her worries, and her dreams for escape.

She said she felt the fly was listening and would react. Sometimes sitting quietly. Sometimes flying around the cell as if to cheer her up. Other times it walked around in circles, which she interpreted to mean she should walk with it to get some exercise.

Years later, in her interview, she didn't say, "Wow, I was totally nuts at that time!"

She thanked the fly for giving her love and companionship during those terrible days.

You know what she could have said? "I prayed for help and companionship, but it never showed up. All I got was suffering in a cell with an annoying fly buzzing around."

She let reality give her something to work with to sustain her. We work *with* life, not against it. We assume loving intent. We align with the energy already flowing through us and around us, knowing that the universe is not a machine to control, but a field of potential that responds to how we show up within it.

Nothing is happening in isolation. Who you are today is an example of "inter-being." You've been shaped by your ancestors' choices, your upbringing, your body, your environment, and the systems you live within. These forces influenced your beliefs and your life experiences. You already carry so much of humanity with you, including your family, your environment, and everyone who's had an impact on you along the way. They've all influenced your ability to create and receive the "feel-good" life you want.

Manifestation, then, isn't about commanding the universe to give you what you want. It's about *collaboration* with the parts of it that support your desires. The most radical heroic act you can take in this life is to see yourself as a beloved and vital part of reality.

You exist in connection with the entire cosmos, and your breath, your actions, and yes, your thoughts, affect it.

HOW TO LEARN WHAT REALITY IS SAYING TO YOU

When you are seeking your goals, tapping into your subconsciousness can be an amazing help. Our quiet mind can tell us what actions to take next. Our subconscious awareness may be connecting those "inter-being" strings and the interconnecting pieces and probabilities.

Even Einstein, one of the most extraordinary brains in history, found that he needed help from some greater part of his consciousness.

Einstein's "Twilight Time" Naps

Einstein would take regular naps. But he wouldn't sleep for too long. He would hold a pencil in his hand so that as he drifted to sleep, it would drop and wake him up. That way, he wouldn't fall so deeply asleep that he wouldn't be able to remember what he learned during this "twilight time," in between conscious awakening and unconscious sleep.

During those twilight nap times, he would do thought experiments like imagining what would happen if he chased a beam of light and caught up to it. These thoughts and ideas allowed him to escape into a "world of pure imagination" (sing it with me). He even said that having imagination was more important than having intelligence.

Thomas Edison, Nikola Tesla, and Leonardo DaVinci are all known for using "nap time" as a way to channel past the conscious mind into the creative super-consciousness.

That twilight moment between dreaming and waking is called *hypnagogia*. You've experienced it, I'm sure, when the alarm clock wakes you from a dream, and you're somewhere in between awake and asleep. It's a creative and imaginative state to notice what's on your mind and what's going on in your body. This is valuable information and can lead to insights that won't come if you're sitting at a desk tapping your forehead, saying, "think, think, think" when you're stuck.

One way I get into this state is through mindfulness time. I set a ticking kitchen timer for 18 minutes (I don't know why I picked 18 minutes, but it works for me) and do calming breaths while I let my mind clear and drift. When the timer goes off, I will often "come to" consciousness in a creative frame of mind. I'll usually keep a journal or something to write with to catch what I notice. Many parts of this book were aided by my twilight time thinking/imagining.

Also, it's a great way to wake up your creative energies, access your imagination, and regulate your nervous system all at the same time!

Your Manifestation Process

What is your desire?: Take a moment to notice what's on your mind right now. What desire, goal, or problem is taking up space in your mind? Don't judge it, just name what it is.

State your Belief: Write down one new belief that would help you move toward your desire. For example: Instead of "I'll never get ahead," try "Every success and failure is getting me closer to my desires."

Check Your Inner State: How does your body feel when you think about this desire? Does your chest tighten or your breathing get shallow? Do you feel a shiver of excitement? Think of these feelings as your nervous system giving you data.

Shift Gently: Now, take three slow breaths. Exhale longer than you inhale. Take a beat in between inhales and exhales. Feel the outcome of the desire fulfilled.

If you notice blockages to this state of being, adjust a part of it and try again. For example, if you notice when you think, *By this time next year I'll be married*, and you feel a heaviness in your chest, ask what that means. If it feels like a blockage, seek out the meaning.

This is where you may want to find a therapist or counselor to talk through things like childhood experiences or traumas that are blocking your expectations for the thing you desire most.

Take Action: Do something aligned with that belief.

You may not know what to do, so you may need to establish a mini-desire.

For example, *My desire is to make a million dollars*, but you immediately realize you have no idea how to accomplish this feat. You can set up a new desire, like *My desire is to attract my attention to new ways I could make a million dollars in the next year.*

Set up a Reminder: Wear a bracelet or ring, set up a timer on your phone or calendar, anything to remind you to regularly get into your Twilight state to check in on what to do next.

I get gung-ho about a desire and quickly get distracted by the next shiny thing. I'll simply forget as life gets busy.

I'll go about my life doing the mundane stuff (I call it "the washing of the dishes" part of my life) and zone out on manifesting my desires.

TIME: THE GREAT DREAM KILLER

For most of us, patience runs thin while we wait for our

desires to manifest. In moments like this, it helps to remember that it's not that things are taking so long, but that the interconnections leading to your goals and dreams are still being formed. They may need to take shape outside of your awareness. Maybe a certain event needs to occur to set in motion the domino effect that will bring things your way. Or you may not be ready for what's to come and need some more preparation time.

It can be frustrating to wait, but our lived reality exists in the dimension of time. While we're waiting for our goals to be realized, we still have to get up and go to work or school, buy groceries, rest with our favorite shows or hobbies, and get the dishes done. We aren't actively pursuing our goals all the time; most of us can't be.

Life continues, and there's a rhythm to that.

There are steps you can take to build your resilience so that the waiting time becomes about creating stability, healing, and confidence. You might still be feeling the pain of your past, responding to your not-so-great environment, or struggling with your genetic and family legacies. You may still have to wrestle with the things that are Not Your Fault.

That's what we'll explore next — how to build a foundation strong enough to feel good, heal, and truly bounce back. This foundation will powerfully support your manifestation work and keep you feeling happy and heroic in the day-to-day of your life. It's called the 6 Building Blocks for Resilience.

6

Introducing the 6 Building Blocks for Resilience

Between stimulus and response there is a space. In that space is our power to choose our response. In our response lies our growth and our freedom. – Viktor E. Frankl

As I left you at the end of the last chapter, I was talking about the time we spend waiting for our dreams to come true. You've set your desire and adjusted your beliefs, you're acting as the hero of your life, "inter-being" with reality, seeking information for what actions to take next. But nothing seems to be happening yet, and you're still dealing with the big and little things in life, some of which bring you down. There's something you could be doing during those times to build up your reserves and feel good while you're going through your quest.

You get to be the Decider in your life. You decide if you want to step into the role of Hero. Between the things that happen to you (the stimulus) and how you react (your response), there is a space. In that space, choices, beliefs, attitudes, and actions are formed.

Maybe you wake up in the morning feeling like an imposter, that everyone else has it figured out except you. Or you look around and see that everyone seems to have a loving group of friends or family while you feel left out. No one wants to live their whole lives with these kinds of unresolved feelings. Nor should they.

We all need time for introspection and healing, and those times make us stronger. But saying, "You'll get stronger" is meaningless until someone shows you *how* hard times actually make you stronger.

That's what the Building Blocks for Resilience are for. Resilience is the ability to bounce back from adversity. It allows you to stay even, balanced, and hopeful while you face challenges.

This is a good time to ask yourself this essential question: *What do I need to bounce back from?*

Maybe you don't feel safe; not in your home, not in your neighborhood, not at work or school. Maybe you've been trying to tell people what you've been through, but no one seems to listen or care. Or you've never learned how to handle your anger or anxiety. Some patterns have been following you for what feels like your whole life, no matter how hard you try to shake them.

I like to say that resilience is the ability to be on your own side when circumstances seem to be lined up against you. If you're going to be your own best friend and stand up and give yourself what you need, you may want some guidance and a foundation. You'll need something you can stand upon and feel secure and anchored to, especially during difficult or chaotic times. That's the Building Blocks.

THE BUILDING BLOCKS START IN CHILDHOOD

Having the Building Blocks is essential for children when they are growing up. I actually created them as a teaching tool after doing some intensive study on child development. I didn't make up the elements of the Building Blocks; child development experts identified the needs they represent. I had just never seen them listed all together in one place.

Here's what's really interesting: Some or all of the Building Blocks were missing in the lives of children who were experiencing the most ACEs and trauma.

But, if you got the Building Blocks growing up, they could protect you from emotional, mental, and health problems later in life – *even if you had* ACEs.

That means they are *preventative* (if you have them, you are less likely to have ACEs) and they are *protective* (if you had adverse childhood experiences, they could protect you from some of the worst outcomes).

The Building Blocks give us a guide to how to develop ourselves into happy, focused, and kind adults. If you didn't get what you needed growing up, you can give yourself what you need now. That's what it means to be resilient. It's about being your own best friend, giving yourself what you need, no matter what you're going through. The Building Blocks are the essence of self-care.

THE BUILDING BLOCKS FOR RESILIENCE

Think of the Building Blocks as the emotional infrastructure of your life.

1. **Protection:** Safety from harm, healthy boundaries, reliable information, and protective environments.

2. **Relationships:** At least one caring, responsive connection with another person.

3. **Belonging:** Knowing you are part of a group and are accepted for who you are.

4. **Coping Skills:** Tools to process stress that feel good now and help you feel good later.

5. **Confidence:** Relying on your personal values and self-trust so you can do the scary things that get you closer to your goals.

6. **Storytelling:** Being able to talk about what happened to you, making sense of adversity, and reframing your story as heroic and meaningful.

WHO GIVES YOU THE BUILDING BLOCKS?

As children, we need a foundation to build our emotional lives. But when we are little, we can't give them to ourselves. How can a child be expected to make their world safe and build their own resilience? Resilience-building skills are for adults to provide. Unfortunately, many parents didn't get the Building Blocks they needed when they were growing up — making it difficult to provide them to their own children. And, admittedly, some people are just not meant to be parents. After doing the work I do with kids in the juvenile dependency system, I say, "Just because you can create a child doesn't mean you can care for one."

Here's why I do the work I do: If we provided these six elements for children growing up today, we could massively change the outcomes for happiness and mental wellness for an entire generation.

Let me give you an example. See if you can spot the ACEs and the Building Blocks others were able to provide to Constance, a poor girl growing up in wealth and privilege.

Story: Constance's Neglect

Constance grew up with a wealthy family. Her father was a successful real estate developer, and her mother was a stay-at-home mom who suffered from many illnesses. Because her mother was sick, Constance was often alone or looked after by a housekeeper, who treated her as a task to take care of, not a child who needed care.

When Constance needed love and attention, it wasn't to be found. One day, she ran out of the house to chase a cat in the yard and almost got hit by a car. No one at home even noticed. She was fed, clothed, and sent to school, but no one said, "How are you feeling today?" or even "How is school going?"

As she got older, she wanted to make friends. But she had no people skills, because at home her parents rarely spoke to her, except to tell her what to do. She didn't feel very confident about herself, so she didn't try new things.

One day, a teacher noticed that she had a vivid imagination. Constance, in her loneliness, had become good at imagining friends and playmates and would create elaborate stories about what they did. This teacher, Ms. Stewart, saw talent in Constance's writing, but she also saw a scared and isolated child. Ms. Stewart invited Constance to have lunch with her in her classroom so Constance wouldn't have to eat alone, or worse, deal with the mean girls who taunted "poor little rich Constance."

Ms. Stewart would ask Constance questions about her life. She let Constance tell her the stories she had made up. Over time, Constance learned from Ms. Stewart how to approach some of the girls in her class and make friends. Ms. Stewart would praise Constance's essays to the class, building Constance's confidence in herself and her abilities. Her teacher helped Constance find an after-school club for budding writers. There, Constance was able to join a group that accepted her and gave her the friendships and connections she missed in her lonely home.

We can see that at home, Constance missed getting and learning about love, affection, protection from harm, friendships, and confidence in her abilities and talents. Ms. Stewart was able to give some of these things to Constance and helped her find the skills she needed to open up her world and start building a foundation for a fuller life. Under her teacher's attention, Constance bloomed. Maybe Constance didn't get *all* she needed from Ms. Stewart, but the reality of life is that most of us rarely get everything we need in childhood. For a good many people, having a difficult childhood is their Origin Story.

But if Constance had not gotten the attention she needed from Ms. Stewart, her lack of protection, relationships, and confidence might have sent her on a bad path. Constance may have sought out drugs, abusive relationships, and negative attention-seeking behaviors in order to get those needs fulfilled. Or she may have continued dissociating from life.

In ways she may never have fully realized, Ms. Stewart provided Protection, Relationships, Belonging, Confidence, and Storytelling, enough to change the trajectory of Constance's life.

Thankfully, we have neuroplasticity and can change and grow from virtually any circumstance. But it's not easy. Nevertheless, the Building Blocks can be put in place at any stage of life. Our motto at Bounce Back Generation is: "If you didn't get them then, you can now!"

How Bad Childhoods Create Life's "Villains"

It's well understood that when people don't get what they need in childhood, it can create adults who seek to fulfill those unmet needs in unhealthy ways. For some, they develop negative personality traits like lacking empathy or exhibiting narcissistic and even psychotic behaviors. Of course, there are other factors at play, like genetics and other environmental influences. But research shows that people who didn't get what they needed in childhood often become adults who take out their dysfunction on the world around them. In fact, some studies show that 97-98% of people in prison had ACEs. Yet, not everyone who experiences trauma becomes harmful to others. Many become deeply empathetic, resilient, and compassionate. When trauma is combined with power, lack of accountability, and reward for aggression and dominating behaviors, the outcomes can be destructive. When trauma is combined with what are called "protective factors," like the elements in the 6 Building Blocks, a life trajectory can be turned around.

Here is where we can collectively "evolve" toward a different future. We can influence many factors that impact children. For example, we can help them train their nervous systems so they don't commit violent acts out of an out-of-control fight response. We can help them to see how their genetic makeup affects their moods and thought patterns, and how generational trauma patterns can be broken. We can help create environments in our society — from schools to online platforms — that support healthy development.

Yet, we currently don't take those "protective measures." Instead, our society seems to promote dysfunction.

We've established that individuals who experience multiple ACEs, such as abuse or neglect over a long period of time, may have a reduced capacity for empathy later in life — and they often seek power as a way to compensate. Unfortunately, our economic systems often reward those who are lacking in empathy, and who can seek out power and money with no care for others.

Several recent studies have shown that while narcissism and even psychopathic behavior can look like strong leadership, they actually destroy organizations. Think of any bad boss you may have had. What makes them bad? Their so-called leadership style is all about keeping people on edge and dysregulating their workers' nervous systems. They create environments that promote an atmosphere of survival rather than resilience. Also, think back to *Chapter* 2, on techniques that hijack our nervous system and how readily those tactics are used by politicians, propagandists, and pundits.

When it comes to our physical health, we spend an enormous amount of money fixing illnesses caused by ACEs and stress, rather than promoting the elements of the 6 Building Blocks for children, and for adults. The ACEs research is clear, children who grow up with dysfunction, abuse, neglect, and unhealthy conditions, if left untreated, often carry their scars into adulthood. We know the outcomes of ACEs are mental health issues, emotional dysregulation, and an increase in diseases like diabetes, heart disease, obesity, drug or alcohol addiction, sexually transmitted diseases, and mental health problems that can lead to suicide. ACEs are bad for our health.

Why do ACEs make us sick? Because being treated poorly or not getting the basics a child needs makes us search outside of ourselves for ways to stop the pain, feel better, and fill the needs that were not fulfilled. We know that an out-of-balance nervous system (one that is stuck in hyper-vigilance for danger and always revved up for fight or flight) feels awful. So we compensate. We drink, we do drugs, we rot on the couch, we eat too much. We take on risky behaviors like looking for love in all the wrong places with all the wrong people, or looking for drama to hide from past trauma. These are expected responses by our brains and bodies to not getting the care and attention we need. The 6 Building Blocks simply try to replace what was missing and build a pathway to self-care. The effects of having the 6 Building Blocks can create generational changes because when parents are better able to care for their children's needs, the child is more likely to grow up with resilience tools.

Can we imagine a world where we finally understand that childhood abuse, neglect, and chaotic environments don't just shape how a child feels — they shape the adult they become, and the desperate ways they try to cope?

In that imagined new world, would we look at a person without a home and drive on by, blaming them for not having their act together? *Or would we wonder what happened to them?*

Would we call a political leader who weaponizes fear "great"? *Or would we explore why they are deliberately trying to hack our nervous system?*

Would we see corporate leaders who prioritize shareholder profits over the well-being of people and the planet as "powerful"? *Or would we see them as criminally trying to profit from harming people?*

And would we tolerate cuts to children's programs, knowing that the bill always comes due in addiction, illness, lost potential, and incarceration?

This is at the root of what I call our emotional evolution. Our ability to evolve differently, on purpose, through understanding that the science of feeling good is vital to our individual and collective futures. It also means recognizing that when others feel bad, they can spread their negative feelings throughout our society. Wouldn't we look then to prevention and healing as pathways to reducing crime, violence, and social harms?

HOW THE BUILDING BLOCKS WORK

The Building Blocks work by helping you identify what was missing and find healthy ways to fulfill those needs now, consciously.

You *deserve* to have all of your foundational needs met.

Do you believe that is true, or is there something inside, maybe your "kryptonite," a belief, that says, *I must have done something to deserve this?*

The Building Blocks and Your Beliefs

Read these statements and see how they sit with you.

Protection: "I am safe in the world."

Relationships: "I am worthy of love and connection."

Belonging: "I have a place here."

Coping Skills: "I can handle difficult times and emotions."

Confidence: "I stand up for myself while I'm learning new things."

Storytelling: "My life has meaning."

How the Building Blocks Support Each Other

These six elements don't exist in isolation. They reinforce each other. Strong boundaries (Protection) make relationships safer. Healthy relationships give you the courage to try new things (Confidence). Belonging gives you an audience for your trauma-to-resilience story (Storytelling). As you strengthen one Building Block, the others grow stronger too.

Think of how each of these Building Blocks might help you right now. But also recognize that the Building Blocks are skills you can learn to help others. If you know someone who has been through something traumatic, the Building Blocks can show you how to help them. They can help you raise your children, or help you provide some support to a kid you can see needs it.

Imagine how the 6 Building Blocks might help someone who has just been through a natural disaster, or a refugee from a war-torn country, or someone who has just experienced the tragic loss of a loved one. Can you provide safety (Protection)? Be a loving friend (Relationship)? Give them a place where they are accepted (Belonging)? Help them find ways to cope (Coping Skills)? Support them as they take their next scary steps (Confidence)? Can you simply listen as they talk about what happened to them (Storytelling)?

If you are ever unsure about how to help a friend through a tough time, think about giving them the elements of the Building Blocks.

WHERE TO START

If you're reading this and thinking, "I don't have ANY of these Building Blocks," don't worry. You don't need to build all six at once. Try just one or two.

Usually, Protection or Relationships are good places to start. Protection gives you the safety to begin healing. Relationships give you support for your journey. As you strengthen one Block, you'll find the others become easier to build.

If you're not sure where to start, ask yourself:

Which Building Block, if I strengthened it, would make the biggest difference in my life right now?

Which Building Block feels most accessible to me right now?

Which Building Block am I most curious about?

Take your time. The Building Blocks are meant to be developed to support you for a lifetime.

The Building Blocks aren't a to-do list or a self-improvement checklist. They're a way to get to know yourself and learn what you need to set up a strong, stable foundation for living.

Whether you're in the "washing the dishes" phase, waiting for your big goals to manifest, or actively going through a traumatic period, the Building Blocks will help you gain strength and feel good day-to-day.

In the next chapters, we'll take each Building Block one at a time and show you how to build what you may have never been given.

7

The Protection Building Block

"*No is a complete sentence.*" — Anne Lamott

Protection is the foundation of all resilience. Without safety, nothing else can be built.

If you are injured in the middle of a road, the first thing rescuers do is move you to safety so you aren't further harmed and proper care can begin. You can't form healthy relationships, explore your potential, or pursue your dreams if you're constantly in an unsafe space or stuck in survival mode.

Protection isn't just about physical safety, though that's crucial.

It's also about:

Emotional safety (knowing you won't be shamed or attacked)

Boundaries that are respected

Environments where you can be yourself

Being able to trust in your own judgment about what is safe and what is not

Access to reliable information so you can make informed decisions

Many of us grew up in environments where protection was inconsistent or absent. Maybe your home felt unpredictable. Maybe adults didn't respect your boundaries. Maybe you learned that saying no led to punishment or guilt trips. Or no one told you the truth about what was going on.

If you didn't get protection as a child, you can start to give it to yourself now. This Building Block is about teaching your nervous system: "I can protect myself. I am safe."

WHAT PROTECTION LOOKS LIKE IN DAILY LIFE

You have a space that is yours, where you can be at peace.

You are able to say no without guilt.

You know what is good for your body, mind, and spirit and

can guard them from harm.

You remove yourself from situations that feel harmful.

You regularly check in with yourself.

You seek out reliable information and can recognize misinformation, manipulation, or dishonesty.

People who respect your boundaries will usually honor your responses. But some people will push back, like the story of Diane and her pushy dad below. If they do, it may be because they really want to see you or be with you, which is nice! But this tactic is also used for control. You have the right to have your time and space respected; always remember that.

Story of Diane and the Dinner Invitation

When Diane was growing up, her father was a perfectionist. He never spanked or yelled at anyone in the household, but he wanted things a particular way. If they weren't, he would scold and lecture while walking closely behind Diane or her sisters and barge into any room to confront them about doing their chores properly.

Diane always felt on edge. The moment she heard her father's car pull into the driveway when he came home from work, her whole body would contract, like a turtle pulling into its shell, as she braced for the verbal nitpicks and space invasions.

As she got older and moved out of the house, her father

mellowed a bit in his old age. He wanted the company of his daughters and would call Diane at all hours of the day with last-minute demands: "Come to dinner tonight. Your sisters will be here."

Diane would scramble, cancel her plans, and show up stressed. Then feel resentful. Then feel guilty for feeling resentful.

After learning about the Protection Building Block, she tried something new. Next time her dad called, she said, "Let me check my calendar, and I'll call you back in an hour."

Her dad pushed. "What do you need to check? Just come."

Diane stayed firm. "I'll call you back in an hour."

In that hour, Diane checked in with herself: *Do I actually want to go? Will it be fun or will it drain me?*

She called back: "I can't make it tonight, but I'd love to see you this weekend. How about Saturday?"

Her dad was annoyed at first. But over time, the dynamic shifted. Diane stopped being the person at the mercy of her father's demands. She became someone whose time and boundaries were respected.

As she gained confidence, she set more boundaries. She finally revealed she had a fiancée named Samantha, and invitations should also include her. Observations about her messy car were also not open for discussion. She was shocked when her father said both were totally OK with him.

When Diane stopped overextending herself and showing up resentful, she had more genuine energy for time with her father, which included talking about how stressed out she felt growing up. He was defensive, she stood her ground, and over time, he began to see her perspective. Diane realized that setting boundaries doesn't have to destroy relationships. They can make authentic relationships possible. If they don't, we'll talk about that in the next chapter on the Relationship Building Block.

In this case, Diane's boundaries made the connection safer.

THE PROTECTION BUILDING BLOCK AND YOUR BELIEFS

Remember from *Chapter* 4 that beliefs shape reality? If you struggle with Protection, examine your beliefs.

Try on these beliefs and see how they fit:

- My needs matter just as much as everyone else's.
- People who respect me will respect my boundaries.
- I deserve to be treated well simply because I exist.
- Saying no to what drains me means opens me to yes to what nourishes me.
- Protecting myself is an act of strength and self-respect.

As you practice the tools in this chapter, you're not just changing behavior; you're rewiring the beliefs underneath. Some days you'll honor your boundaries perfectly. Other days you'll slip back into old patterns. That's OK. It's about progress, not perfection.

One Caveat: I know people whose boundaries are *too* strong. They use boundaries and “you must respect me at all times” as a way to keep people back and avoid intimacy.

Protection is necessary, but we also need to consider letting people in. Let’s look at how we form relationships in the next chapter. Because once you can protect yourself, the next step is to let people in safely.

8

The Relationship Building Block

If you want to go fast go alone. If you want to far, go together. — African Proverb

Humans are wired for connection. Neuroscience suggests that feeling socially isolated turns on some of the same brain regions that register physical pain.

We don't just want relationships; we need them. But you don't need dozens of friends or a huge social network to build up your Relationship Building Block. You need at least one caring person who really sees you, accepts you, and shows up for you.

Research on resilience consistently shows that having just

one close relationship in childhood with a parent, grandparent, teacher, friend, or mentor can act as a buffer to the effects of trauma and adversity. That one person can set you up for a lifetime of good feelings and positive beliefs about yourself.

I've seen this so many times. A child's home life is terrible, but there's a next-door neighbor who lets them "run away" to their house for hot meals, a hug, and help with homework. I've worked with kids who have a parent who is incarcerated, and a loving aunt or grandparents step in. Some kids never knew what it was like to live in a stable, loving home until their coach took them under their wing, providing understanding and guidance.

But many of us still didn't have that person growing up.

You are worthy of the love you need. Why do I know this about you? Because everyone is worthy. Every person on Earth needs at least one person to see them in their light and darkness. It's just how we are built. This building block is about learning *how* to build connections with others, even if you feel uncomfortable letting people see the real you.

WHAT GOOD RELATIONSHIPS LOOK LIKE IN DAILY LIFE

There are no perfect relationships. So knowing what makes a good relationship, even when they aren't always doing what you'd like or need, is helpful. The main problem many of us have is not knowing whether the relationships we have are good for us, are holding us back, or are not what we need them to be.

What does it mean to have a good Relationship Building Block (remember, not a perfect one)? Just having one of these situations can make a world of difference:

You have at least one person who really sees you.

You feel safe being yourself around certain people.

You know you can reach out when you're struggling.

You experience "Serve and Return" over time in conversations (more on Serve and Return below).

You feel seen, heard, and valued.

You can be vulnerable without fear of judgment.

You can give and receive support.

BUILDING A STRONG RELATIONSHIP

Most of us need help to figure out how to make a relationship work. Sometimes we don't even know where to begin with someone we're into. Sometimes we can get confused about whether to leave a relationship or just cool it down for a while.

This next tool is helpful for building, maintaining, and knowing when to leave a relationship. It's not the only tool. You will need to consider the other person. What is their communication style? Are they shy? Are they going through something stressful?

Nevertheless, knowing the Serve and Return process can be a great place to start.

"Serve and Return"

Serve and Return comes from child development research and describes how babies learn to communicate and build trust with their parents or caregivers. It's like a game of tennis. A baby coos or smiles (that's a serve). The other person responds with eye contact and words, sounds, or actions (the return). This back-and-forth lights up the child's brain with pleasure and excitement. It's proof that they can reach beyond themselves and have an impact on another person.

As adults, this knowledge works in a similar way. Instead of "goo goo ga ga," you'll be saying, "Hey, this thing happened today. Do you have time to talk about it?" and be able to take it from there.

Steps to Serve and Return:

Serve = You share something real

Return = They respond meaningfully

Example of good Serve and Return:

You: "I'm feeling anxious about this presentation tomorrow."

Them: "That sounds stressful. How are you holding up?"

They received your Serve and they Returned with something meaningful. The conversation can continue.

Example of poor Serve and Return:

You: "I'm feeling anxious about this presentation tomorrow."

Them: "Oh." (Checks phone.) "So anyway, did you see that new show on Netflix?"

They didn't Return. The ball dropped. It's not awful that they want to talk about the show on Netflix, but you've reached out for something deeper.

Some people are not sensitive to what you need, and that's why Serve and Return is not just lobbing a ball toward them and them hitting it back. It's about gathering information about how deeply they can respond to your meaningful conversation. There is nothing wrong with saying, "Yeah, I saw it, but right now I want to talk about this presentation. Can we talk? How do you deal with the stress of having to do public speaking?"

If they aren't able to be responsive to that request, then you may need to move on and let it go.

This doesn't mean you give up on the relationship, but you've got some information about how deeply you can speak to them about the things that are most important to you.

Serve and Return doesn't need to happen in perfect lockstep with every conversation. It's more of a pattern over time. Are both people engaged and invested? Does it feel balanced? Also, Serve and Return isn't just verbal; it's about actions too. If you say, "I'm feeling anxious about this presentation" and the person you've served puts a hand on your shoulder or hugs you, that's a Return!

You don't need to keep a scorecard, but if you feel like the effort is always one-sided, that's information for you to consider.

Meeting New People: Starting the Serve and Return

If you're trying to build a relationship with someone new, Serve and Return helps gauge their interest and compatibility with you. Remember, it's not about whether you're worthy of a relationship; it's just that some people are going to be compatible and others aren't.

You sit next to someone at a party: "Hey, I'm Marcus, mind if I sit here?"

Good Return: "No, go ahead. Hi, my name is Vanessa. Who do you know at this party?"

She's engaged. The conversation can continue.

Poor Return: "Go ahead, sit where you want" (turns to talk to someone else).

Game over. She's not interested in connecting right now.

Or she's feeling shy. Or she was in the middle of a deep conversation with someone. This isn't rejection, it's just information. Not everyone is available for connection at every moment, and that's OK.

If you already have friendships you would like to deepen, using Serve and Return can help carry conversations forward. Think about using these techniques to encourage confirmation about what a relationship means to you and the other person. This is what we call setting up your "In Case of Emergency Person."

Setting Up Your "In Case of Emergency Person"

You know how on forms, like for school, work, and doctor visits, you designate someone to call in case you're incapacitated? That's your official "In Case of Emergency" contact person. In the context of relationships, your "In Case of Emergency Person" (ICEP) is someone you've made an explicit agreement with to be there for specific needs you might have.

Here's how to set this up:

Think about someone in your life who really gets you. Maybe you don't see each other often, but every time you talk, you feel seen and heard. You always end the conversation feeling better about yourself.

Say something like this:

"I really value our friendship. I always feel great after we talk, and I hope I can do the same for you. I want you to know that if you need to talk or something difficult has happened, I'm here for you."

They might say the same back. Now you're each other's ICEP for "when something difficult has happened." This doesn't mean it's an iron-clad contract with each other, just that you're asking and telling each other what you need or hope to receive.

Here are some important clarifications you should consider. Just because they said they could be there if you needed to talk doesn't mean they are also going to be the right person to call if your car breaks down at 2 a.m. That may need to be someone else. It also doesn't mean they're available 24/7 or that they'll drop everything every time. That's OK. Check in with each other and signal what you can offer.

The power of making this explicit:

Making it explicit, having the conversation, prevents resentment and mismatched expectations. Many friendships or romantic relationships stall because one person thinks the relationship means something the other person doesn't think they've signed up for. This doesn't mean the other person doesn't love or care about you. Some people have other things going on, things that may be overwhelming them, and they *can't* commit to being there for you.

Remember the Protection Building Block — you may be the

one who is not able to be there in the same way for the other person. You may be dealing with things in your life, or you may not feel the same connection. That's all OK. The main thing is to be clear about what each of you needs without creating unrealistic expectations.

Suki and Lakshmi: A Friendship Story

Suki and Lakshmi met when they were paired as roommates in their college dorm. They became friendly and talked a lot about classes and people they were attracted to, and a little about family life at home. They were growing closer when Suki had tragic news: Her mother was sick and in the hospital.

Suki left school to be with her mother and asked Lakshmi to help her collect her assignments from teachers, keep friends updated, and be her liaison with the dorm. Lakshmi was happy to support her new friend.

Time went on, and Suki's mother was not improving. Suki continued to try juggling being there for her mother and staying in school, often flying back and forth between home and campus.

One day, Suki sat down with Lakshmi and said, "I wanted to say thank you for being there for me all of this time. I see that you are the kind of person I would want to build a real friendship with because I can see how caring you are. I want you to know that I can be the same kind of friend to you. Let me know if you ever need me to help out with anything, or just to talk."

That was a powerful moment in their friendship because they were able to define what the relationship meant to them.

They've been friends ever since. They were there for each other through Suki's mother's passing and Lakshmi's painful breakup with her boyfriend during grad school. They now live in different states but talk almost daily through texts and phone calls.

Lakshmi later admitted that until that moment, she was coming very close to feeling used by Suki. She didn't know if Suki really appreciated her beyond the quick, breathless thank yous as she rushed off to the airport or hurriedly ended phone calls.

That conversation set up their friendship as meaningful to both.

Think about what would have happened if they hadn't had that talk. Lakshmi, being kind and no-drama, might have slowly stopped responding to Suki's requests. Suki would have felt betrayed by a friend, and Lakshmi would have felt used.

Does Gender Matter in Developing Deeper Friendships?

I just told a story of two women having a relationship and the need to define who they were for each other. For guys, this may not feel as easy. I'm over-generalizing here because I've seen plenty of men open up with their feelings and have great, lasting friendships. But it may be helpful for some to see how Serve and Return might work to gain deeper male relationships — or deepen any friendship that has always been "surface."

Here's a scenario:

Darnell and Luis: A Deeper Friendship

Darnell and Luis have been friends forever. They hang out, play basketball sometimes, and that's all good — until something serious happens.

One afternoon after work, they were shooting a quick game when Luis had some news. He'd lost his job. He was laid off to make room for AI. What scared him wasn't just being unemployed. It was the thought that he might never find work in his industry again.

He needed to talk.

Darnell: "Hey, what's up?"

Luis: "Bad news. I just got laid off."

Darnell bounced the basketball and stood there for a moment, trying to figure out what to say. Did Luis need to vent? Did he want help finding work? Encouragement? A distraction?

Darnell went with encouragement.

Darnell (bouncing the ball, eyeing the hoop): "You'll find

something. You always do."

Luis wasn't sure how much he could ask for. He *did* want to talk things through. But was Darnell open to that? Or did he just want to play the game and head home?

Luis took the safe route and assumed Darnell just wanted to play.

Luis: "Yeah. Thanks. I hope so." End of conversation.

But, Luis really needed more from his friend.

Now imagine a small adjustment on both sides.

Instead of guessing what Luis needs, Darnell simply asks.

Let's rewind and replay that moment.

Darnell: "Hey, what's up?"

Luis: "Bad news. I just got laid off."

Darnell: "Damn. Do you want to talk it out? That's scary, especially in this economy."

Luis: "Yeah, actually. I'd appreciate that. Maybe after the game we can hang out. I need to think through next steps, and I'm pretty worried."

Sometimes friends just need you to listen. Sometimes they need advice. It sounds like Luis needed both.

Now, Darnell might be thinking: *I really don't have the bandwidth today. I was just up for a game.*

One-on-one conversations can feel intense for some people, too intimate. That's why sometimes you'll find that friends will avoid that kind of closeness. That's where finding things to do together, while talking, can be a great way to have Serve and Return conversations.

Maybe you can go play a game of tennis, or even throw a ball back and forth while talking, which can lower the intensity of the interaction.

I know of an 11-year-old who was in the foster care system and was adopted. At first, the dad/son relationship was very hard to establish. The boy was not used to talking about himself. He'd been through a lot and was closed off and scared.

One day, his new dad asked if he wanted to throw a baseball around in the front yard. The kid agreed. As they were throwing the ball back and forth, the dad asked simple questions like "How are you liking your new school?" The boy answered, and as they tossed the ball back and forth more questions and answers came up. Over time, conversations became more meaningful. The boy was able to talk about what had happened before his adoption and how he was feeling now. Serve and Return was working – and because they were doing exercise, it had the added benefit of releasing physical stress and calming both of their nervous systems.

Serve and Return can be done while sitting next to each other in a car on a road trip, on a phone call, or while taking a hike together. I find that the best conversations I have are while I'm cooking for someone as they sit watching and chatting with a beverage. Even a text or email exchange where I can fully lay out my feelings and know the other person is able to read and respond thoughtfully can be a very satisfying Serve and Return moment.

I learned a powerful line from someone I know who has a lot of friends who lean on her. You can borrow it too if you're not sure how to show up for someone who says they need to talk:

"Tell me what you need from me. Do you want me to just listen, or do you want my feedback and advice?"

You can also set parameters like, "I've only got a few minutes, but I really want to focus in on what you're saying."

It's not weak to want someone to just listen. And it is not a male thing or a female thing. It's just human.

What to Do When Your Nerves Get in the Way

I think most people have experienced really wanting a relationship with someone and being terrified of rejection. Finding and building a relationship often means getting your nervous system through discomfort. There are two things you can do:

1. Never approach them. Just crush on them from afar, or

2. Think of what you have in common and start a Serve and Return conversation.

Check in with your nervous system, do your calming exercises, and remind yourself: Regardless of the outcome of your attempts to get close, you deserve love and safety. It may be from this relationship, or it may need to come from someone else. I know this sounds simple, and it really is, even when your feelings feel complicated. If you find yourself having to chase, force, convince, or bend over backwards, maybe it's not the relationship for you?

You do need to protect yourself, so asking questions and taking time to learn and observe how they handle things is vital to building a safe relationship with someone.

If you are manifesting a relationship, it's important to see the difficulties you encounter as *information* the other person is providing to you. That means listening to reality when it is telling you what the relationship *is*. I know, this is hard when you have a desire and vision of *what could be*. If you're unsure about whether your relationship is right for you, listen to your friends. Talk to someone you respect who has wisdom about love. You can still decide you see something they don't, but it's always good to get feedback. Don't go it alone.

One thing to be aware of is how sex can distort our feelings. Sex releases a surge of oxytocin, which is known as the bonding hormone. Oxytocin can make someone feel "in love" even when they barely know the other person. It can even make them think there's an instant attachment, like they're instant soulmates. But that's our evolutionary blowback to get us to build a fast connection with someone so they'll stick with us and help raise the resulting offspring. Those intense feelings can be powerful, confusing, and even a little blinding. When you understand it's just hormones doing what hormones do, you can slow down, breathe, and decide whether the relationship itself is actually healthy, not just chemical.

THE RELATIONSHIP BUILDING BLOCK AND YOUR BELIEFS

If you struggle with this building block, try on these new beliefs:

I am worthy of love and connection.

I don't have to be perfect to be loved.

Some people will leave, but the right people will stay.

It's *normal to need connection.*

Building relationships when you've been hurt takes courage because you can't control other people. So ...

Having intimate one-on-one relationships feels, well, intimate. One-on-one relationships can make you feel vulnerable, open to being hurt, and sensitive to the other person's reactions to you. Many, many, many of us struggle with these issues! You're not alone. So, maybe *that* relationship, or any relationship, is too much right now. Maybe you want to try being part of a group. One that understands you, first. Then move inward to find that single friend or significant other.

That's the next chapter, where we explore Belonging.

9
The Belonging Building Block

"*We are Groot.*" – Groot

Throughout the movie *Guardians of the Galaxy*, the character named Groot only says three words: "*I am Groot.*"

He had no backstory to explain what that meant. He was just "Groot", an alien identity.

But near the end, when everything is crashing around the *Guardians*, Groot realizes he's part of something larger, a motley group of misfits from around the Galaxy. As he lies mortally wounded, having sacrificed himself to protect his companions during an intense battle, his sidekick, Rocket, asks in anguish, "Why did you do it?" Groot says, just as he is about to perish, "*We are Groot.*" He did it out of love for his friends.

I admit, I shed a tiny tear in that moment. I warned you, I'm a fan of the commercialized superhero movie genre.

But the larger picture here is: Isn't that what we're all searching for? That moment when we go from "I" to "we?" That feeling of being connected, even at one, with others? That's the feeling of belonging.

In the last chapter, we talked about Relationships, the intimate, one-on-one connections you have with people who are caring and responsive to your needs. This chapter is about something related to that, but different.

Belonging is about community. It's the feeling that you're part of something bigger than yourself. It's knowing there are people like you in the world. It's having a place where you fit in.

Relationships are close, intimate connections like your best friend, your partner, your parent, your sibling, your mentor.

Belonging is group membership, including your community, your tribe, your family, or clan. It's your people.

And, we need both.

WHY DO WE NEED TO BELONG?

Let's go back to the cave for a moment. Without each other,

our ancient ancestors were doomed. We needed a group or tribe to support each other. Imagine being left out on your own on a desert scape or the cold tundra to battle the elements, find food, and fight off predators.

Being cast out for any reason was often a death sentence, unless you could find another group that would take you in. Our brains are evolutionarily wired for belonging. It's normal to want to be included, and it is painful to be left out.

Today, being left out of the school clique or the after-work hangouts isn't a life-or-death matter. But it still hurts. If a young person tells me they didn't get invited to the party and everyone else got to go, I feel their pain almost like it was happening to me (and I want to march over to that kid's house and say to everyone there, "How dare you!"). It's that powerful for us to want to be connected.

HOW TO FIND WHERE YOU BELONG

So, where do we belong? What if your school, work, family, or friend group leaves you on the sidelines all the time?

If this is happening to you, it's time to find a group that lets you in. Look for people who are like you. You're not different, you are *unique*. Do you have unique interests? Are you neurologically unique (like ADHD or on the spectrum)? Are you physically unique? Do you have unique hobbies or interests? Are your habits and ways of looking at the world unique? I can pretty much guarantee that whatever makes you unique, there is a group for you somewhere.

We say a lot of bad things about the internet and social media, but one thing that can be positive (with some warnings I'll talk about below) is that you can find an online group for just about anything. You can also start a group of your own.

There was a time (and still is in many places) when being gay was extremely isolating. Now, there are rainbow groups and subgroups everywhere, not just online, but in many communities, in person. Look to your school, your local clubs, find websites, magazines, Reddits, and Substacks where you might find like-minded people.

There are groups for people who like anime and video games. There are groups for people who are really tall and for people who are big. People get together who have unique animals (snake lovers, parrot lovers, and calico cat lovers, the list is endless), groups for people who have been through a tragic event (9/11, Katrina), groups who are against violence, or love books of a particular genre, or like to bake bread. For some, it is their family, clan, or neighborhood. I could go on, but you get the picture.

HOW TO BUILD UP YOUR BELONGING BLOCK

Sometimes we spend years trying to belong in spaces that will never fully accept us, like a workplace that doesn't value us, a family dynamic that rejects our identity, or a social group that makes us feel "less than."

It's worth asking if you're doing something either intentionally or unintentionally that is blocking you out of the group. I've heard of reasons like:

"We all really like Yosef, it's just that when we are hanging out, he interrupts people and gets loud if they don't listen. I don't think he knows he does this."

Or, "Lyric has never fit in because she's just too young. We don't feel like we can have her hanging out with us because we're doing stuff that may not be age-appropriate for her."

You have the right to ask, "Hey guys, you all went out yesterday for lunch and didn't ask me. Is there a reason I should know about?"

Yes, that's a super uncomfortable conversation, but it's good to have the information. Remember in the chapter on manifestation how important it is to gather information? The answer may be as simple as, "*We went to that steak place, and since you're a vegetarian. We thought you wouldn't want to come.*" Or it might be that they don't think you fit in.

Whatever the answer, it's okay to find your people elsewhere. Many people have had to leave their family of origin behind because they weren't accepted for who they are. They form a secondary family, a family of choice made up of friends. That's valid, too.

Sometimes we overlook the communities we're already part of. Think about it:

- Just gave birth? You're now part of the "new parents" community.

- Military veteran? You belong to the veteran community.

- Cancer survivor? There's a community for that.

- Love random music no one else likes? Someone, somewhere, likes it too.

- Enjoy reviewing movies online? That's a community.

- Adopted? Trans? Neurodivergent? Immigrant? First-generation college student? These are all communities.

The key is, if you identify a group you could belong to, you want to actually do things with them. It is important to participate. Belonging isn't just about receiving; it's also about giving.

The Value of "The Nod"

Sometimes belonging doesn't require formal groups. It's about recognizing our shared humanity. It can help the new kid or the person stranded in a scary situation feel less lonely.

I've noticed a powerful practice among African Americans. It's a nod, just a small tilt of the chin between Black people, especially in predominantly white spaces. It's a way of saying, "I see you. I'm here for you." African Americans have succeeded in ways that show their extreme resilience, including the ability to form belonging even in places that are not safe.

We can all learn from this practice to create strength through shared experiences and connections. These micro-moments of recognition build a felt sense of belonging to the human family. You don't need words. You just need to show: *I'm just taking a sec to say I see you.*

Story: *Carter and the Book Club*

Carter was lonely. He'd moved to a new city for work and didn't know anyone. He tried going to bars, but it felt weird to sit alone. He tried dating apps, but found them exhausting and disappointing.

One day, he saw a flyer at the library: "Science Fiction Book Club - First Thursdays."

He almost didn't go. He thought: *What if they're all way more well-read than me? What if I don't fit in?* But he went.

It was awkward at first. He didn't talk much. He mostly listened. But he was a bit of a science nerd and was fascinated by sci-fi depictions of futuristic technology. After a few meetings, he started sharing his thoughts about whether they were realistic or possible from a tech standpoint.

People started asking, "What did Carter think about that chapter?"

When the group went out together on days they weren't meeting for book club, Carter joined. He became a solid member of the group. He'd found his people.

Belonging can take time. You have to show up, be patient, and let the connections build naturally. You might feel awkward at first. That's normal.

BEWARE OF THE DARK SIDE OF BELONGING

One important note before we continue: there's a dark side to belonging.

Not all communities are healthy. Some groups offer belonging based on negative emotional states. They base belonging on who you don't like, or who you want to harm. That kind of belonging is built on putting people down or excluding others.

White supremacist groups, anti-Semitic groups, and anti-LGBTQ+ groups are *not* examples of seeking community and belonging. They're examples of people who are deeply insecure and searching for people to feel superior to in order to gain a false sense of personal power. Remember the section on bullies? It's the same dynamic, only amplified, with more people.

This is the opposite of personal power. It's weakness and fear masquerading as strength.

True belonging doesn't require anyone else to be "less than." True belonging says: "We accept you as you are. You have a place here. We don't exclude; we invite."

If a group requires you to hate, exclude, or harm others as a condition of membership, that's not belonging; it's a cult or hate group.

Another warning that we will talk more about in the next chapter is groups that practice unhealthy coping skills. You can belong to a fun group and realize that maybe the only reason you get together is to get drunk or overuse drugs. You might encounter groups that are supportive of unhealthy lifestyles, groups that promote anorexia or bulimia, or that fantasize about suicide. You're not coping in these groups. You are amplifying your dysfunction and harming yourself and each other.

THE BELONGING BUILDING BLOCK AND BELIEFS

Building belonging when you've felt like an outsider your whole life is a heroic act of courage. You're teaching your nervous system: *There's a place for me in this world.*

Everyone deserves a place to belong. Remember: you don't need to belong everywhere. You just need to belong somewhere.

Try on these new beliefs:

"There is a group out there for me."

"I don't need to fit in perfectly to belong."

"I can join a group and keep my boundaries in place if they ask too much of me."

"If this group doesn't work out, I'll eventually find the right one."

With the Building Blocks of Protection (safety), Relationships (intimate connections), and Belonging (community) in place, you're building a foundation from which to face tough challenges.

In the next chapter, we'll explore the fourth Building Block: Coping Skills. Because life will throw difficult things your way, and you're going to need the tools to handle them.

10

The Coping Skills Building Block

"*A good coping mechanism helps you feel good today, and better tomorrow.*" — Bounce Back Generation.

When you were growing up, did anyone teach you how to cope when things went sideways?

Yeah, me neither.

Some Gen Z and Gen Alpha kids tell me they learned skills in school through social-emotional learning tips, like breathing exercises, counting backwards before responding, and making good choices. But most of us learned through observation.

Growing up, we saw people light up a cigarette, down a cocktail, or smoke a joint when stressed. We observed how coming home from work was an opportunity to release stress on everyone. We saw that running away from problems was an option. We learned to ignore huge problems to "keep the peace."

We did learn coping skills. But they weren't always good ones.

WHAT MAKES A GOOD COPING SKILL?

A good coping skill makes you feel good right away AND helps you feel good later, too.

That's it. It's that simple.

If feeling good after work means downing a six-pack, but tomorrow you drag yourself out of bed with a headache, it's a coping strategy. But not a good one.

If scrolling social media for three hours numbs your anxiety tonight, but then gets you involved in some online beef. Not good.

If screaming at your partner releases your stress in the moment but damages your relationship, obviously, not a good coping skill.

Good coping skills meet both criteria: they reduce stress NOW and don't create new problems LATER.

WHAT COPING SKILLS LOOK LIKE IN DAILY LIFE

When the Coping Skills Building Block is strong:

You have tools to calm yourself when stress levels spike.

You know what helps you feel good today without making you feel worse tomorrow.

You don't rely on destructive habits to numb yourself or escape.

You can regulate your nervous system.

You recover from setbacks relatively quickly.

You have multiple coping tools that are personal to you.

You can choose the right tool for the situation.

YOUR COPING TOOLKIT

When stress hits, have a list of things that genuinely help you feel better. Think of it like an emotional tool box you can reach into when you need something to get you through a rough situation.

You'll want to make sure that what's in your toolkit works for you. You don't want to pick things you think *should* help because they work for someone else.

Some women, for example, swear that a day at the spa getting a facial and mani-pedi is a great way to de-stress. I find it boring. Others might think climbing El Capitan in Yosemite is a great time. I find it terrifying.

You have to personalize your stress release. For me, baking cookies, reading a good book, or watching a movie with my cats and dogs around me is a perfect way to unwind. I'm sure for many that sounds very old lady. What can I say, it works for me!

We are all different in how stress impacts us, but usually a good de-stressor involves your mind, body, and emotions. That's why the Tattoo from *Chapter* 3 is a great place to start.

Here are some other ideas to try:

Walk around the block

Call a friend

Dance to a song in front of your mirror

Journal for ten minutes

Take a hot shower

Watch funny videos

Pet your dog or cat

Rearrange your furniture or do a small decorating project

Listen to your curated chill playlist

Do something creative (draw, knit, play music)

Hit the gym

Daydream

Massage your pressure points on your face and neck*

Read a chapter of a favorite book

Have a kind, supportive conversation with yourself

Pray

Use "tapping" techniques*

Take a sound bath*

Meditate*

Check in: Did you eat today? Drink water? Stretch?

**On our Youtube Channel @bouncebackgeneration you will find short "Rest and Reset" videos on different techniques like mindfulness, pressure points, tapping techniques, sound baths and more.*

Write down 5-10 things that work for you. Put the list somewhere you can see it. When stress hits, don't reinvent the wheel. Go to your toolkit.

Also, you don't need to do just one. You can combine them. Let's say you've had the worst day at work and you come home with your shoulders up to your ears, feeling frustrated or angry, and mentally exhausted. You might kick your shoes off and stretch on a Pilates roller, put on some music you like, and when you're done, turn on your favorite show. Sounds great.

But, beware! This great coping skill can become not-so-great if you stretch, listen to music, and 8 hours later you're binging your show and it's 3 am.

It's all about balance.

Dopamine Sips vs. Dopamine Hits

Speaking of balance. Our brains do not appreciate being out of balance. What can make a brain "out of balance?"

Our friend, **Dopamine**.

Who doesn't love dopamine? It's the neurotransmitter/hormone that gives us that little spark of pleasure and drive when we move toward something we desire. It's why you feel excited opening presents on Christmas morning, why your mouth waters at the thought of your mom's famous pasta dish, or can get laser-beam focused on making your model ship project.

But not all dopamine experiences are created equal.

Dr. Anna Lembke, in her book *Dopamine Nation*, explains that our brains are designed to stay in a steady state (called homeostasis). Think of your brain like a seesaw. One side goes up (pleasure, yay!), and the other side slams onto the ground. Your brain doesn't like that super high-high. It will automatically try to level things out by tipping the other direction, from high to low. It likes to be in balance.

It's a simple equation: the higher the high, the lower the low.

Here are some examples of potentially big dopamine hits for you that feel great in the moment, but can cause you to crash later on:

- Scrolling or gaming for hours
- Eating an entire cake or the entire bag of chips
- Using drugs or alcohol to excess
- Gambling
- Seeking new experiences constantly, like multiple sexual conquests

You feel amazing during the hit, but afterwards, the other side of the seesaw comes down hard, and you feel the crash. And over time, you need bigger and bigger hits just to feel normal. That's how addiction works. It's a trap! It looks like pleasure, but it really ends up draining your capacity to feel joy. If you have experienced that crash after a big high, you know what follows can be physical exhaustion, depression, feeling hopeless, and desperation to get that high back again.

Long-term use can mean that it takes more and more to get high, or that the pleasure they had from the initial high feels elusive. According to Dr. Lempke, the only way out of this cycle is to stop using. That way, your brain has the opportunity to level out its dopamine.

But we can still seek those dopamine "highs", just in a gentler way. I call them **Dopamine Sips**.

Dopamine Sips are gentler, smaller, more frequent moments of pleasure. Try these:

Daydream for a few minutes

A few squares of chocolate at a set time each day

Headphones on for a short walk with no interruptions

Look at photos that make you happy

Text a friend something funny

Water your plants

Make your bed or organize a drawer

Give yourself a manicure

Spend time in nature

Go for a short drive and park somewhere with a view

Try a makeup tutorial

Reread a book you love

Play a video game (with a time limit if needed)

Savor your first coffee of the morning

A ten-minute meditation after a shower

A walk around the block at lunch

A 4 p.m. tea and text with friends

Three minutes of stretching

Soak in some sun and fresh air

Take a short nap

Sit in your car and rock out to one good song while you breathe and decompress

What are your dopamine sip ideas?

Think of dopamine sips like raising your pinky from a china cup. They're small pleasures your brain can process without sending you into the overload zone. Small, consistent rewards strengthen the brain's dopamine pathways without exhausting them. That means better mood stability, more motivation, and less crash-and-burns.

The goal is to build a rhythm of pleasure throughout your day using dopamine sips. But wait, there's more!

You've got a little bit of a pharmacy inside you to tap into for more "feel good" boosters.

Your Body Is Your Friend

So far in this book, we've talked quite a bit about dopamine as the chemical that motivates you and rewards you when you pursue something meaningful.

But dopamine isn't the only way your brain and body try to help you feel better. Our ancient evolutionary system is designed to help you survive stress, recover from pain, connect with other people, and maybe most importantly, find balance again – homeostasis. To do this, here are two more assists in your biological internal support team: serotonin and endorphins.

Serotonin: The Stabilizer

If dopamine is about getting you up and moving, serotonin is about being steady.

Serotonin helps regulate mood and sleep, manage impulse control, and support social connections. It's not going to make you wildly excited and jump a couch when something good happens for you. It creates something quieter and more powerful: the feeling that you are okay.

When serotonin is functioning well, you might notice:

You're generally calmer. Calm is your baseline mood.

You're less reactive when something unpleasant happens.

You have more patience.

You feel connected more easily and have a stronger sense of belonging.

You sleep better.

The way to get more serotonin into your chemical mix is actually by doing simple, practical things:

Get some sunlight. Move your body more. Set up routines so you get more sleep. Eat well. Hang out with friends (that give good Serve and Return!), and do something that helps you feel connected to others, like volunteering or helping out someone who needs it.

Unlike dopamine, serotonin is undramatic. It's just small, steady measures you take.

Here are some more ideas for how to keep your serotonin pumping:

Going for a regular short morning walk.
Keeping a regular sleep schedule.
Helping someone.
Spending time with one safe person.
Reflecting on being grateful instead of comparing your situation with others.

A TikTok Example

I follow an older woman on TikTok who was recently widowed. She was feeling lonely at night, so she started making TikToks for her small audience every evening. She would sit down in a comfortable chair, with her dessert. It was a ritual she used to do with her husband every evening. They'd have dessert and talk about their day. On her TikToks she would show what she had made for herself that night, like a small bowl of warmed-up apple pie. Then she would talk about her day, remembering good moments she had with her husband.

The widow said the likes and comments helped her not feel so alone and she would sleep better. She would get DMs from followers who had lost a spouse too. Or people would wish her a good night and sweet dreams. She made a little serotonin-boosting space for herself and others. She also created a Belonging Building Block space.

She didn't need to go viral or have a million views. In fact, I think if that happened, it would be awful because — that's the internet. Someone would eventually say something nasty. But, she's fine with her small, intimate audience of good night well-wishers.

What the TikTok lady knew was this: she knew herself. She had the wisdom to seek out something she needed rather than sit feeling lonely every night before bed. She sought out gentle feel good moments be reenacting a soothing ritual she had with her husband.

Endorphins: The Pain Buffer

Now let's talk about endorphins.

Endorphins are the body's natural pain relievers. They are opioid-like chemicals your brain releases during physical stress or strong emotional experiences. They help you push through hard times and soften painful moments.

How do you know you're getting endorphins? Think about how you have felt after a really deep and intense fit of laughter. It's that breathless but almost euphoric feeling of relief after a laughing jag. Crying is another way. A deep, good cry can leave you feeling a calm exhaustion that lets some of the emotions go. I sometimes seek out movies I know will leave me weepy because I feel like it lets me release emotions I'm not fully in touch with.

Remember in the chapter on *Taming Your Nervous System*, we talked about how your body needs a "finish line?" Releasing endorphins is part of that. When you've been tense, frozen, or overwhelmed by a stressful event, your muscles are often holding that stress. Movement, laughter, and even tears allow your body to complete the stress cycle and reach that finish line so your body can regain its equilibrium. Think of endorphines as pressure valves.

If you have just gone through an intense emotional experience and it needs to be released, try these coping mechanisms:

Exercise with some intensity.

Watch a comedy that leaves you in stitches, belly laughing

Watch a movie or read a book that gives you a chance for an emotional cry

Sing or chant

Dance

Sit with someone you have a strong bond with. Even if you don't speak.

Some people swear by cold showers (careful, though, about cold plunges as they can be dangerous for some).

The key to all of the inside chemicals we have to assist us with coping is to know what works for you.

Story: *James at the Gym*

James had been "trying to get back to the gym" for three years. He'd buy a membership, go for a while, and then slowly taper off. He knew exercise was supposed to be a great way to boost his mood and help him live a healthier lifestyle. But he spent more time beating himself up for being lazy and undisciplined than he spent at the gym.

One day, feeling especially annoyed and uninspired, he asked himself: *Does the gym actually make me feel good?*

He sat with that question and finally realized: *Honestly? I hate the gym. I feel self-conscious. I find it boring and kind of torturous. Everyone says they feel great after working out, but I just feel relieved that it's over.*

Then he asked himself: *What actually makes me feel good?*

The answer came immediately:

A hike with his dog Spike

Playing tennis with friends, and hanging out after

Riding his bike to the café to get coffee in the morning

Talking to his mom after a hard day

James canceled his gym membership and started doing the things he actually enjoyed.

Within a few weeks, he realized he was getting more exercise than when he was forcing himself to go to the gym. He was in better shape, not just physically, but emotionally. He felt happier, more connected to his body, and less stressed. Calling his mom more regularly also boosted *her* mood and serotonin levels.

Your coping skills have to work for YOU. Not for Instagram. Not what some podcaster swears by. Not what your friend does. Just what makes you feel good today, and just as good (or better) tomorrow.

WHAT IF YOU CAN'T STOP?

Ask Someone Who Knows

Coping mechanisms often turn into addictions. If that happens, my advice is: get help. I can't say this enough. Serious addictions are not something most people can handle on their own, nor should they.

Think of it this way: Millions of people have gotten addicted to something, whether it's prescribed pills or street drugs, food, or doing compulsive behaviors like hoarding. Millions of people have also kicked their addictions, and most of them had some kind of help from people who have either been through it themselves or know how it's done.

Take advantage of those who have come before you to tell you the best, easiest, and least painful ways to stop doing what you know is harming you. At the end of this book, you'll find resources you can reach out to for help.

The Replacement Process

The second way to handle addictive coping skills is to replace the destructive ones with constructive ones. It's called the Replacement Process.

Step 1: Identify the need that the destructive coping mechanism is meeting.

Examples:

Scrolling for hours: numbing anxiety, avoiding difficult feelings

Drinking to excess: relaxing after stress, numbing pain

Overeating: comfort, distraction, pleasure

Step 2: Choose a healthier tool that meets the same need.

Examples:

Numbing anxiety: ten-minute meditation, a walk, or journaling

Relaxing after stress: warm shower, stretching, music (remember the vagus nerve)

Comfort and pleasure: put on soft PJs and set aside time to call a friend or watch something funny

Step 3: Practice the new tool repeatedly.

It may feel awkward at first. That's normal. Your brain is used to the old pattern. Give the new pattern time to take hold.

COPING AND YOUR BELIEFS

If you struggle with this Building Block, try on these beliefs:

• "I can learn to handle stress in healthy ways."

• "Using tools to manage emotions is a sign of strength and self-awareness."

• "It's okay to need support. Everyone does."

• "I'm capable of building new, healthier patterns."

• "Good coping skills are a superpower."

COPING SKILLS AS A DAILY PRACTICE

Building the Coping Skills Building Block is ongoing.

• Notice your stress levels before you're overwhelmed by them

• Choose tools that serve you

• Build a toolkit of options

• Practice dopamine sips throughout the day

• Replace destructive patterns with healthier ones

- Be honest about what actually makes you feel good

Building healthy coping skills when you've relied on destructive ones for years is hard work. You're teaching your brain new pathways. That's neuroplasticity at work.

Be patient and kind with yourself.

TAKING CARE OF YOURSELF

This is very basic, foundational information you must be aware of *constantly*.

Eat well, sleep enough, avoid unnecessary risks, and protect yourself mentally, emotionally, and physically – including around sex. Remember what I said earlier: sometimes when we feel bad, there are physical reasons. Hormone imbalances, illness, mental health conditions, or medication side effects can block your ability to feel good. If you're struggling, please go to the doctor.

Please don't assume everything is solved by self-care. Sometimes good coping includes getting help from professionals who know what they're doing. And if you don't get relief from one provider, many insurance plans allow a second opinion. Know your rights. Good coping is not about perfection. It's about giving your future self a better day.

Building Your Foundation

With Protection (safety), Relationships (intimate connections), Belonging (community), and Coping Skills (tools for stress) in place, you're ready to step into your power.

In the next chapter, we'll explore the fifth Building Block: Confidence. Because we could all use more courage to pursue our highest goals.

11 The Confidence Building Block

"Don't be satisfied with stories of how things have gone for others. Unfold your own myth." – Rumi

Most people I know wish they had more confidence. Even people who seem capable and confident will admit they still feel shaky inside sometimes. Or, that they had to face their fears over and over until confidence came.

Here's what most people don't understand about confidence: it doesn't come before action. It comes after.

Even Beyoncé has stage fright. She created her alter ego "Sasha Fierce" to give herself the courage to go onstage. I've read that Adele gets sick to her stomach before her performances. There is an old classic actor named Laurence Olivier who is considered one of the finest of all time. But he would freeze before he had to perform, and someone had to physically push him onto the stage.

Confidence doesn't mean fearlessness. It means doing the thing despite the fear.

I had a friend who was a fantastic singer, but then imposter syndrome took over ("I feel like I'm going to be found out to be a terrible singer."). She almost quit her ambitions to be a performer because she read her fear and lack of confidence as a "sign" that she shouldn't even try. If it was "meant to be," she thought, she'd feel confident enough to jump onstage like a badass.

She discovered she had it backwards. Confidence is built by doing something through fear, not by waiting until your fear disappears. She had to stick it out until she finally felt like she was a badass.

Some people are born with higher levels of confidence (genetics, again), and some have had it built into them during childhood through consistent praise and support.

But even if we've been confident all of our lives, trying something new can leave us with moments of doubt and fear.

The good news is you can build up your confidence. Anyone can, at any age.

COGNITIVE BEHAVIORAL THERAPY AND CONFIDENCE

Cognitive Behavioral Therapy (CBT) is the recognition that there is a connection between your thoughts, feelings, and behaviors. Let's say you are afraid of clowns. A CBT series of sessions might include first looking at a picture of a clown and asking yourself, *Why is this making me scared?* You are challenging a belief you hold, as we did in the chapter on Beliefs.

The CBT process will then present mini-experiments that push you further into the thing you fear, little by little.

Can you watch a short cartoon with clowns? Can you then visit a store where there are clown outfits and so on, until some event, like going to a circus and watching the clowns perform, doesn't freak you out. That's when you'll know you've overcome your clown fears.

By the way, this is a real thing. It's a phobia called coulrophobia, which is the excessive and unreasonable fear of clowns.

The CBT process helps build confidence and, added bonus, shows you how to manage new fears when they come up.

You can do CBT on yourself. That's what I did when I was afraid of driving on the LA freeways. I ventured back onto freeways slowly, with some tweaks (going at off-times, traveling in the slow lane, following a car in front that seemed like they were a safe driver). It worked. But if you have a major phobia, you should find a therapist who specializes in phobias; that's always the best option.

The Confidence Building Block is about having techniques to get you toward building confidence, which is really another way of saying that you've gotten better at managing your fear. We seek confidence so we can do things that are important to us: Ask that girl/guy out, stand up and speak, try a new sport, or start a new job. *What do you want to get confident enough to do or try?*

I'm going to share with you a technique for gaining confidence that has been shown to work with many people.

But first, let's explore:

WHAT CONFIDENCE LOOKS LIKE IN DAILY LIFE

When your Confidence Building Block is solid:

You believe in your worth even when you mess up.

You make decisions based on your values, not other people's opinions.

You take action even when you're scared.

You trust your judgment.

You root your identity in who you are, not what you achieve.

You recover from failure without letting it destroy you.

You try new things even when you're not good at them yet.

HOW CONFIDENCE IS ACTUALLY BUILT AND SUSTAINED

Underneath confidence, you'll often find fear, and as we've learned in previous chapters, what does fear do? You got it: It triggers your nervous system reactions. Now you're afraid. You're a shaky, breathless, heart-pounding, stomach-churning mess.

So job #1 when you're not feeling confident is to get into your "nervous system management mode."

This is where you're going to use the Tattoo or vagus nerve calming methods to manage your triggered reactions.

You may still get a twinge (or more!) of fear or apprehension about what you have to do, even after you've calmed your nervous system. But this is about trying to get into feeling more balanced, not acting like a perfectly calm robot. You're just ratcheting your nerves down a bit.

The next steps are steps you've probably used many times, but were unaware you were using them.

Think back to a time you didn't feel confident, but did the scary thing anyway. Why?

1. Your desire to do the thing felt greater than your fear.

When you learned to walk as a baby, your desire to move and explore was greater than your fear of falling. When you started a sport or tried out for the school play, or ventured out on a trip on your own, your curiosity and desire to try it were greater than your fear.

2. You connected to something you value.

Values are the deepest things we say about ourselves. They are at the core of who we are. You might describe your personality as “bubbly,” “quiet,” or “athletic.” But your values are things you would fight for, like “honesty,” “knowledge,” or “loyalty.”

Having your desire and curiosity merge with something you truly value, along with your ability to manage your nervous system reactions, can be a winning combination when seeking confidence.

When the thing you want to do is rooted in a value, doing it becomes more important than being afraid of failing.

Think about archetypes and the stories about our shared human experiences, like the Hero’s Journey. How many stories can you think of where the person made the ultimate sacrifice or walked through their worst fears because of something they really believed in?

That's why it's important to ask yourself: *What are my deepest values?*

Your Values Check-In

Here are some common values. Read through this list and circle or write down 10 that resonate with you. Then narrow it down to 5. Then choose your Top 3 Values.

Authenticity • Achievement • Adventure • Authority • Autonomy • Balance • Beauty • Boldness • Compassion • Challenge • Citizenship • Community • Competency • Contribution • Creativity • Curiosity • Determination • Fairness • Faith • Fame • Friendships • Freedom • Fun • Growth • Happiness • Honesty • Humor • Influence • Inner Harmony • Justice • Kindness • Knowledge • Leadership • Learning • Love • Loyalty • Meaningful Work • Openness • Optimism • Peace • Pleasure • Poise • Popularity • Recognition • Religion • Reputation • Respect • Responsibility • Security • Self-Expression • Self-Respect • Service • Spirituality • Stability • Success • Status • Trustworthiness • Wealth • Wisdom

When you're feeling shaky about yourself or facing a scary decision, ask:

- What are my top 3 values?

- If I do this scary thing, am I honoring those values?

- What's one small action I can take to live according to my values?

When you live in line with your values, you'll be compelled to do the scary action even if you're afraid. Then, the confidence will come *after* you've worked through your fear.

There are several archetypal story arcs where the hero totally lacks confidence in their abilities. Or they are afraid to use their abilities because they're not confident they can handle the responsibilities of such power. In all instances, they had a moment where they had to line up their values like, "I need to save the world" or "I need to rescue my friends," which forced them to do the act *while* they were terrified, and *before* they had confidence they could do it.

You don't need to feel confident to act. You need to act to build confidence.

Story: *Lin and Her Ugly Art*

Lin had been painting in secret for years. They were strange paintings that included objects she found on the street, things that caught her eye. It was all very personal. No one would understand the artistic connections she made in her mind and tried to express through her work. Lin didn't show anyone. She thought, objectively, her art looked ugly.

She decided to take an art course to see if she could make her work "prettier." A few weeks in, her art teacher challenged her: "What matters to you about making art?"

Lin thought about it. "It's how I process my emotions. It's about my ability to find beauty in things that people think are garbage. It's how I feel seen."

"So your value is... what? Expression? Being seen in a new way?"

"Yes. Exactly."

"Does hiding your art honor that value?"

Long pause from Lin..., "No."

Lin realized she was not being true to herself by hoarding her art. She decided to post one painting on Instagram.

The reception was mixed. Her friends liked it (maybe just to be nice), but there were no comments of encouragement. She felt kind of dumb. *Why am I doing this to myself?* Lin wondered.

But she remembered: she made art to be seen and for her emotional expression to be understood.

So, she posted another one. It was a rock underwater in a dirty pond, with a feather floating on top. The caption read: "The rock is my heart sunk under the weight of trying to be light as a feather." She added a laughing emoji and posted it.

Now she got traction! Friends liking and commenting. They knew that feeling, too.

Not all the comments were positive. People she thought would like it were lukewarm in their praise. But Lin was doing what she valued, what she thought was important. *I'm working on something here*, she told herself.

She felt she was making art for herself first, for her own need for expression. She didn't need everyone else's approval to feel validated. But, she also knew it was part of her mission to be seen, and that meant having her art seen. Part of her art persona, she realized, was to produce work that not everyone had to like.

She continued making art, honing her talents, and learning how to communicate with her audience so they could enter her world and perspective. It's a work in progress that Lin is beginning to really enjoy.

For Lin, checking in with her values helped her have a reason to do the scary thing (to have her work seen, even if it wasn't liked), which she did. That action is now building her confidence.

She didn't wait until she felt confident to post her art. She posted her art. Her confidence will come from doing the scary thing over and over, despite what random people think, do, or say.

The Evidence Journal

Your inner critic is loud and persistent. Your inner cheerleader needs evidence so it can grow stronger. Remember the Bayesian Theory? Your brain will seek out evidence for what you believe.

When self-doubt creeps in, write down three pieces of evidence that show you're capable. These don't have to be huge accomplishments:

- "I had a tough conversation with my boss and stayed calm."

- "I cooked dinner for my girlfriend even though I'm not sure I'm a great cook yet."

- "I helped my kid with homework even though I didn't understand the math."

- "I showed up to the gym even though I know I don't look hot in this outfit."

- "I spoke in front of 10 people even though I was terrified."

Small evidence counts. Over time, you're building a case file: "I did the scary thing."

What are your 3 pieces of evidence?

WHAT IF YOU FAIL?

Sometimes the scary thing doesn't work out for you.

You get excited about doing the community play and opening night, you freeze up, forget your lines, and stand crying on stage. Or, you approach that guy you've had a crush on, and he brushes you off.

Actor Jim Carrey started doing stand-up when he was a teenager and completely bombed. The audience booed him off the stage, and the host of the show said he was boring. Jim Carrey was so freaked out by that experience that he stopped performing for 2 years. But something inside him compelled him to come back, and as they say, the rest is history.

Do this daily or weekly – when the inner critic gets loud, open your Evidence Journal and read it. Remind yourself of what you've already survived and accomplished.

You're going to fail. I'm sorry to say, it's going to happen. That's the story of the hero. They rise up and fall down. They struggle. It's a process.

It takes time, practice, and the ability to bounce back when everything and everyone seems lined up against us. When superheroes are alone, in their crystal cave, their "fortress of solitude," their lonely planet, or sitting in a prison in darkness...they make sure they never forget the values they are fighting for.

"The Action is Greater Than the Outcome" Practice

Most of us measure confidence by outcomes: Did I succeed? Did people like it? Did I win?

But outcomes are often outside your control. You can give a great presentation and still not get the promotion. You can make beautiful art and still not get into the gallery. You can do everything right and still fail.

That's why it is so powerful to make the effort more important than the outcome.

In my book, you're successful if you can say:

- I did the thing I was afraid to do.
- I acted on my values.
- I showed up as myself.

You can only control your actions, not how they're received. So, stop trying to control what others think of you as *the* measure of success. What you think of yourself means more.

Remember from the Belonging Building Block that we carry with us the fear of being left out of the tribe, stranded alone because we did something they didn't like?

That image, of people standing around judging, and that terrified feeling that "they won't like me," is a powerful relic from evolution. It doesn't really work like that anymore. Our world is bigger. The playing field is more diverse. If one tribe is not OK, maybe you can head over across town and try another venue. Even failing online is sometimes just a matter of setting up a new account.

Each time you do the scary thing, you prove to yourself: "I can handle discomfort. I can survive feeling afraid." That's what confidence feels like.

The "Do It Badly" Practice

Perfectionism is the enemy of confidence. It keeps you from trying anything you might not immediately be good at.

Try this instead: **give yourself permission to do things badly.**

Want to learn guitar? Play off tune for a while.

Want to write? Write terrible first drafts.

Want to try a new sport? Suck at it initially.

The goal isn't to be good. The goal is to do it. To take action. To build the evidence that you can try new things and survive not being perfect.

Being willing to be bad at something is a tremendous confidence-building action. I've seen people walk onto a playing field for example and say, "I've never played __________ before, but I'll give it a try." They do their best. They ask questions. They try their hardest.

They still suck. But every famous athlete started off being awful at their sport — or at least not a champion at it yet.

THE CONFIDENCE BUILDING BLOCK AND YOUR BELIEFS

If you struggle with this building block, try on these beliefs:

- "I am enough, exactly as I am."
- "Failure is information, it's not my identity."
- "I don't have to be perfect to be valuable."
- "My worth comes from within, not from what other people think."
- "I can trust myself to figure things out."

Building confidence when you've spent years doubting yourself is an act of courage. You're teaching your nervous system: *I've got this. I can handle whatever comes.* This might be your line when you do the "talk kindly to yourself" part of The Tattoo.

CONFIDENCE AS A DAILY PRACTICE

Building the Confidence Building Block is ongoing. Ask anyone older than you about confidence. They will probably tell you that they feel far more confident today than they did when they were, say, 17 years old. But if they are doing something new and different, they might feel right back at 17 years old, trying to get their courage up. They know they will need to take action despite their fear.

It's All About The Heroic Journey

With Protection (safety), Relationships (one-on-one connections), Belonging (community), Coping Skills (tools for stress), and Confidence (trusting yourself) in place, you have almost everything you need to build your resilience foundation.

In the next chapter, we'll explore the Storytelling Building Block. Because the way you make sense of your life determines how you live it.

12

The Storytelling Building Block

"Stories are among our most powerful tools. They help make us who we are." – N. Scott Momaday

Storytelling is how our brains make sense of life. Neuroscience shows that when we hear a story, our brains light up in the same areas that would activate if we were actually living that story.

Hearing a story puts us into the story. I've lost myself in books and movies and "come to" feeling disoriented, like I'd left that world and landed back in mine.

Stories help us organize our experiences. When something difficult happens to us, our brain scrambles to make sense of it. Storytelling gives our brain a framework.

You know what the framework looks like because you've seen it so many times: a beginning, a middle, and an end. Where does your story begin? What's happening now? Are you at the end, or did something happen that starts a new storyline?

Storytelling helps us take chaotic memories and painful emotions and organize them into something that makes sense. Psychologists often use techniques that help us shape our experiences into a narrative. It's a way to take raw emotions and understand (and often transform them) through reflection. That shift helps regulate our nervous system, too.

Think of it this way: telling the story helps you step out of the emotional alarm system and into the part of you that can observe, understand, and choose. That distance creates objectivity.

Remember the Charismatic Pause? Instead of instantly judging what happens as "good" or "bad," you pause and assess before acting. You could also use the technique of the Chinese Farmer. You don't rush to label an event good or bad; you realize the story isn't over yet.

And as we learned in the Manifestation chapter, the way you interpret reality influences the actions you take next. Those actions then shape where the story goes — either closer to or away from your ultimate goals.

Storytelling is how you turn "*what happened to me*" into "*this is how I choose to use it.*" You become the author and interpreter of your life, not just the person blindly reacting.

For example:

Did you ask someone for a date, and they rejected you, and they were the 5th person who has said "no" to you? Is that the end of the story?

"I'll never get into a relationship. I'm going to stop even trying."

Or is it the beginning of a new storyline?

"That was the day I decided to take a deeper look into why I kept failing when it came to dating."

The story you tell about your life will shape how you live it.

What Storytelling Looks Like in Daily Life

When the Storytelling Building Block is strong, you:

You make meaning from your experiences.

You see your struggles as part of a larger journey, not random punishment.

You connect your story to archetypal patterns (see below for a list of archetypes to consider).

You find purpose in your pain.

You reframe setbacks as plot twists, not as endings.

You see yourself as the hero of your story, not the victim.

A Note on Trauma and Storytelling

If you're sitting on a memory or experience that's too painful to talk about, please consider seeking out a professional to help you process it. Therapy, especially trauma-informed therapy (therapy that helps you work through your trauma without feeling like you have to re-live it or feel re-traumatized), can provide the safe container you need to walk more gently through "the scary forest" of that memory. That process can be very healing. That's why storytelling can be one of the most powerful tools for resilience.

Practicing the Storytelling Building Block

The Story Check-In

When you feel stuck in a negative story, pause and ask yourself:

What story am I telling about my life right now?

Is it a story of victimhood?

Life is against me. Bad things always happen to me. I'm cursed.

Is it a story of heroism?

I've survived so much. I'm still here. I'm becoming who I'm meant to be.

Is it a story of stuck-ness?

This is just how it is. Nothing will change. I'm trapped.

Notice the narrative you're living in. In my experience, a good story contains all of the above. Sometimes we are victims and people are awful to us. Sometimes we are heroes, and even heroes get stuck. That's reality. The point is, you're the author of the story.

The Reframe Practice

When something painful happens, try reframing it through an archetypal lens:

Instead of: I lost my job. I'm in a panic. I'm a failure.

Try: *I am being forced to take a new path. I'm going to focus on what I really want to do next. It's in these kinds of moments that I discover what I'm really made of.*

Instead of: My relationship ended. I'll be alone forever.

Try: *I'm shedding old skin. This is an Origin Story moment for me. Something new is coming.*

Instead of: My creative projects aren't getting the attention I wish they would. This proves I'm not good enough.

Try: *This rejection is redirecting me toward something better. It's giving me a chance to dig deeper into my work.*

You're still allowed to grieve, get mad, and feel pain.

The Reframe doesn't erase all your suffering; it just helps you find a way out of it.

Your Legacy

When you're in a crisis, or things are just not going your way, ask yourself:

"If I were telling this story ten years from now, what would I want to say about how I handled this moment?"

This pulls you out of immediate reactivity and into a larger perspective. Don't force these feelings. When you make the statements in the examples below, just try them on and see if they feel empowering. But if they don't, or you're not ready, that is perfectly OK.

Examples:

• "I want to say I kept going even when it was hard."

• "I want to say I asked for help instead of suffering alone."

• "I want to say I chose to stick to what I value over giving in to peer pressure."

• "I want to say I survived and became stronger."

Using Archetypes - Humanity's Patterns

Archetypes are timeless patterns wired into the human psyche. You know them well. They are characters like the Hero, the Healer, the Rebel, the Villain, the Sage, and many others. These characters mirror our inner world and remind us that our struggles and transformations are universal.

When we see ourselves in these archetypes, we realize: "I'm

not lost. I'm on a path others have walked before."

Here are some common archetypes you might recognize:

• The Hero (Luke Skywalker in Star Wars, Katniss in The Hunger Games)

• The Mentor (Dumbledore in Harry Potter, Mr. Miyagi in The Karate Kid)

• The Trickster (Loki in The Avengers, Jack Sparrow in Pirates of the Caribbean)

• The Villain (Darth Vader, Voldemort)

• The Innocent (Frodo in Lord of the Rings, Big Bird from Sesame Street)

• The Rebel (Han Solo, the kids from Stranger Things)

• The Sage (Gandalf, Yoda)

You might identify with multiple archetypes at different times in your life. You might be the Hero in one area and the Innocent in another. You might have to face your inner Villain (the part of you that wants to give up or hurt others).

The way archetypes work is that we all have these sides of our personalities inside of us, and they can come out when summoned ("bring forth my Rebel!") or recognized ("that was the wise Sage in me talking").

Using archetypes helps you understand that your life is a vital part of a larger human story. As we learned in the chapter on manifestation, your actions are constantly inter-being within the world. Our actions and observations are part of the cosmic connectivity we all share. Everyone's life matters and matters a lot.

THE HERO'S JOURNEY TEMPLATE

Your life is a quest. It's a powerful journey where you discover your talents and powers and how they fit into the world.

There's something inside of you that is here to be expressed. The Hero's Journey template helps you see what it is and how to hold on to it, even when the journey gets rough.

1. Origin Story: The Traumatic Beginnings

This is where your journey starts. Most heroic journeys begin with something painful or confusing, or a great loss. This could be your childhood trauma. A major life disruption, or a big moment that changed everything.

You probably didn't choose this origin story. It's usually part of something that is Not Your Fault. Either way, it is still a new starting point, not the end of the story.

2. Unknown Powers and Secrets

We all carry secret thoughts about ourselves. Either things that were not right about our lives (abuse, dysfunction, an illness, extreme poverty) or secret powers we believed we had but didn't feel we could reveal ("I've always had a secret dream to be a train conductor. I don't tell anyone about it. They wouldn't take me seriously.").

For some of us, we may not understand ourselves well enough to even know how to dig out what that secret *is*. Secrets can lie in buried belief systems or be covered by shame or other difficult emotions that we feel we cannot face.

3. Mentor or Sidekick

Along the way, you search for and find someone to confide in and trust with your secrets, or someone who becomes a helpful guide. This could be a family member, coach, teacher, therapist, friend, or even a book or online community.

4. Kryptonite

You become aware of the things that drain your strength. Bad habits, addictions, negative thought patterns, toxic relationships, or limiting beliefs. You learn how to avoid or overcome them.

5. Honing Your Superpower

This is a period where you must learn how to build your powers, manage them, and feel confident about using them.

You are spending this time training, studying, learning, practicing, failing, and trying again and again.

6. Who Do You Save?

At some point, you feel ready to use your powers. You decide or learn who you have the capacity to save. It can be yourself, your family, or simply one person who's going through what you went through. It can be the world, or the generations to come. It can simply be that your joy, success, and happiness are contributing to this world's overall positivity. You can be providing an evolutionary contribution to this planet's good future.

Your story is meaningful, and even your pain can serve a purpose. That purpose might be how to avoid pain in the future, or help someone else avoid pain, or better, find joy.

You may find that in the end, your superpower is related to your origin story and finding a way out of the adversity or trauma you had to experience. It's the way we can use our tragedies and turn them to triumph, and struggles into strengths.

Because great heroes do not seek suffering, they overcome it. They do what they can to prevent the unnecessary suffering of others and by doing so, help themselves and others to feel good.

Story: *Bruno and the Cancer Diagnosis*

See if you can spot the elements of the Hero's Journey in Bruno's story.

When Bruno learned he had cancer, it was a new and traumatic **Origin Story** for him. Bruno was facing an aggressive but treatable cancer. He would have to embark on a journey through tough treatments, not to mention the mental and emotional anguish of this terrible news.

Bruno kept a **Secret** he would have to face. Part of him felt responsible for the cancer. He searched for all the things he did to "deserve" getting sick. The years he smoked. The times he drank and ate junk. The cheap place he chose to live near the industrial plant. He blamed himself. But to everyone else, he put on a brave face.

Bruno joined a cancer survivor support group, and the leader talked about how people often internalize blame for getting sick. Bruno felt relieved. He wasn't the only one who felt that way. In the group, he connected with Manuel, a guy around his age, with the same type of cancer. They became friends, going out with their wives in between treatments. They went bowling, out to dinner, and took short weekend trips. Bruno felt lucky to find his **Sidekick** in healing.

But negative thoughts dogged Bruno: “Why should I be one of the 75% who survived? What if I live and Manuel doesn't? Or the opposite?”

He went back to the group leader for help and asked, "How do people deal with these kinds of thoughts?"

The group leader told him that thoughts of shame or guilt were common. They stemmed from feelings that we must "make deals with God." That we're undeserving and must prove our worthiness. He told Bruno, "Your survival rate has nothing to do with Manuel's. You don't have to bargain your suffering against others to be worthy of healing."

Bruno started examining his beliefs (his **Kryptonite**). Why did he think his health and happiness meant others had to suffer? He realized he'd never questioned this belief. He was taught he was sinful and didn't deserve anything unless he sacrificed everything.

He decided that it didn't make sense. Why couldn’t both he and Manuel be worthy of health and healing?

Bruno battled to overcome the negative beliefs that were

hurting his recovery. He continued treatments and eventually started to get some positive news that the treatments were working. During the long stretch where his health was always on his mind, he realized so many people struggled with thoughts that arise when sick, and how much they impact the healing process.

Bruno had always been a good talker with a great "radio voice." One day, he created a podcast called "I Deserve to Heal." It was a steep learning curve. Bruno could talk, but he was no genius with microphones, cameras, and editing. His first few episodes were obviously amateurish. But he stuck with it. He was **Honing his Superpower**.

Over time, Bruno's treatments ended and he got indications that he was in remission. So was Manuel, who became a guest on his podcast.

Bruno got really good at podcasting, and the podcast became a place for people struggling with serious illnesses to build a positive healing mindset. His experience and the skills he built gave him a superpower: supporting thousands of people on their healing journey.

Bruno's Hero's Journey helped him, and now he is helping others. Other cancer survivors like him are — **Who he Saves**.

Your Hero's Journey

Take some time to map out your own Hero's Journey:

1. What's your Origin Story? What trauma or challenge

shaped you?

2. What Secrets do you keep? What are things you don't talk about? What power do you hide?

3. Who is your Mentor or Sidekick? Who helps you along the way?

4. What's your Kryptonite? What drains your power? How are you learning to overcome them?

5. How are you Honing your Superpower? What are you practicing? What are you becoming good at?

6. Who do you Save? Who benefits from your journey? How does your pain become a purpose?

You don't have to have all the answers yet. Your story is still being written.

The Storytelling Building Block and Your Beliefs

If you struggle with this Building Block, try on these new beliefs:

- "I can make meaning from my experiences."
- "My past shaped me, but it doesn't define me."
- "I'm the author of my story, and I can write and rewrite each chapter."
- "My story matters to me, and potentially to others."
- "I'm the hero of my own journey."

Building the Storytelling Building Block when you've felt like a victim of random suffering is deep and profound work. It happens over time. I am still working and reworking my own hero's journey. Believe me when I say there are days when I do not feel like a hero. I feel like a victim, I feel like a rebel, I feel like a fool.

The Hero's Journey takes contemplation. You need to sit with yourself and take the time to focus on what things mean to you. This is where meditation, or using your Einstein-like Twilight Time, can be really helpful. Use your imagination. You're the author of the story. The only person who can tell your story properly is *you*.

You've now learned all six Bounce Back Generation Building Blocks for Resilience:

Protection → "I am safe in the world."

Relationships → "I am worthy of love and connection."

Belonging → "I am connected to others."

Coping Skills → "I can handle difficulty."

Confidence → "I trust myself to live by my values."

Storytelling → "My life has deep meaning."

You've gained some life-changing tools. These are tools that science has uncovered by studying how our brains and bodies work. Your brain and emotions, your nervous system, and your psychology want to be in balance. They want to function well and keep you safe.

You've learned that we all start with circumstances that are imposed on us, like our nervous system, genetics, childhood experiences, and environment. They shape our lives in ways we cannot always control. That's not your fault, but you are not powerless.

You've learned how to manage your nervous system and use plasticity to change your mind, and in doing so, change your experiences. You've questioned your beliefs and begun to create new ones. You've learned that manifestation is your ability to observe and play with reality, interacting constantly with what *could be*, turning it into what *is*.

You've gained the Building Blocks for Resilience to help you bounce back from what happened to you in the past, and to stand powerfully upon those blocks as you move into the future. You've learned that you have the privilege to evolve your own emotional life, and in doing so, influence the future of all humanity.

But there is one thing we haven't talked about — and we should before you end this book:

Your emotions.

13
Emotions and Feelings

"Sometimes I think I need a spare heart to feel all the things I feel." — Sanober Khan

I shared an early draft of this book with our youth staff at Bounce Back Generation, and a few of them asked me, "When are you going to talk about feelings?"

At first, I was surprised. I thought I had been talking about feelings, especially feeling good. But they were right. They weren't asking about feelings as a concept. They were asking, How do I actually deal with my emotions when they show up in real life? It's a great question.

So far in this book, I've focused on immediate nervous system reactions (fight, flight, freeze, fawn, or faint), which are emotional responses as much as they are automatic biochemical responses.

We begin to emotionally evolve when we recognize what's happening as our nervous system is triggered.

It can sound like this: Oh wow, I'm in fight-or-flight because this salesperson won't let me return this sweater.

As I've talked about in this book, once we notice that, we can work with the reaction using tools we've learned by slowing our breath, moving in ways that relax our muscles, and helping our nervous system return toward calm before we speak or act. That shift also helps us move back into our thinking mind.

But that's only part of the story.

Feelings are how we experience these reactions. As our chest tightens or our face feels hot, we may want to argue, cry, or escape. Those sensations show up as feelings like anger, frustration, shame, or guilt. In better circumstances, emotions can also appear as excitement, connection, power, or love.

Let's go back to the return counter where the lady won't let me return my sweater.

I might notice my fight response rising and experience it as irritation or feeling disrespected. This is so unfair! The woman behind the counter says I can't return the sweater, even though it's unraveling and it was expensive!

If my nervous system shifts into flight, I might feel embarrassed or invisible, suddenly wanting to leave the store as quickly as possible.

And if I freeze, it might be because something about the interaction brings up an old memory. Maybe the cashier's tone reminds me of how my mother used to scold me.

This is why learning to work with our feelings alongside our nervous system is so important. Our nervous system reacts based on past experience before logic or language arrives on the scene.

Instead of pushing feelings away or shutting them down, we can recognize them and look for their deeper meaning.

When you're in the middle of an intense feeling, ask yourself: *What is this experience really telling me? What past experience am I bringing into this moment?*

When we look beneath our feelings, we often find fear or love at the root. If you keep gently asking, *What's underneath this?* You may hear something deeper needing to speak up:

I need to be understood. I need to express myself. I need to be seen. I'm afraid. I want to feel safe.

These internal conversations that dig deeper, past fight or flight, are acts of love for ourselves. You're creating an internal Serve and Return by taking the time to listen and respond to yourself.

Back at the return counter again. Under my anger might be fear that I wasted money on a defective sweater. Beneath that could be a fear that I don't make good choices in my life.

When I'm willing to go that deep, I can begin to rebuild a positive sense of self with compassion. Maybe I did make a bad choice. I can still offer myself forgiveness or mercy for making the choice to buy the sweater. Maybe the woman behind the returns counter is just doing her job. Maybe the fight isn't worth it. Maybe the fight *is* worth it, but I can stand up for myself in a calm and determined manner.

When you take time to ask, *What does this feeling mean for me?* You're building a relationship with yourself. You're exploring a deeper, sometimes hidden, inner world. That act turns emotions into information. And as we learned in the chapters on **Beliefs** and **Manifestation**, information is what allows us to make life work better.

The **Hero's Journey** and the **5 Factors** help us see adversity, setbacks, and even trauma as opportunities for growth, and not just reasons to blame ourselves or others. We can seek a way to look at a situation that feels good and remove guilt, anger, blame, and shame. We can find solutions that work instead of creating new traumas (or just new dramas) in our lives. This gives us some say and some management and control over our experiences.

The **Storytelling Building Block** helps us reframe what happened, and the other **Building Blocks for Resilience** allow us to heal from the things we didn't get growing up.

Feelings are messengers from parts of ourselves we may not yet know well. That means if you're suffering from long-term emotions like depression or feeling disconnected from life, you're getting even deeper signals that something inside needs attention. Seeing a doctor, finding a therapist, talking with someone you trust, reading, reflecting, or seeking spiritual guidance are avenues to explore.

You are the hero of your life. The work may seem quiet and ordinary. You're just getting through college, raising a child as a single parent, or going for that promotion. But it's extraordinary to pursue your dreams while investigating your feelings, honoring your emotions, and living by your values without harming yourself or others. Those humble actions have the power to heal yourself, improve your relationships, break generational family traumas, support your community, and ultimately be part of an emotionally evolving world.

With the growing scientific understanding of our brains, bodies, and emotions, we can live differently than our ancestors did. We can choose to evolve in ways that create better lives for ourselves and help reset humanity's future.

As you move forward, remember to ask yourself: *What is my body doing? What am I feeling? What might this feeling be asking for?*

Then allow your heroic self, and that spark of resilience in you, to speak back.

Epilogue

What Are We Evolving Toward?

"The most reliable way to predict the future is to create it." — Abraham Lincoln

Remember what we saw from our spaceship floating above Earth in the year 2126 at the start of this book? That future will be possible if we start creating it today. If we look closely, we can see the evolutionary patterns for tomorrow are already forming.

The Human Advantage

While tech corporations tell us the future lies in robotics, bio-implants, and artificial intelligence, it's the awareness of our emotional world that's really the upgrade for the planet. Our ability to regulate our nervous system, heal, think through fear, and tap into deeper human emotions is the future "job."

Machines may evolve to General Intelligence and be smarter than us, but what they cannot do is navigate moral dilemmas grounded in human values, empathy, and the fact that *we* live with the consequences. The person who can slow their breath, calm their body, and respond from values rather than fear will be carriers of the real future superpowers.

Just as our ancestors didn't let the spear decide its target, we cannot let our technologies decide what is right, what is humane, or what is worth protecting. Technology is our tool, not our master.

We are the Deciders.

Our responsibility is not just to build smarter machines, but to keep probing, debating, and refining what it means to be human, and which values we choose to uphold when the decisions are hard.

Dr. Bandy X. Lee, a renowned psychiatrist and expert in the causes and cures of violence, frames the essential question this way: "What biological, psychological, and social forces sustain life and support the survival of the species, and which ones lead toward destruction and extinction?" Machines can assist, but cannot answer this question for us.

I think of *Star Trek* and its recurring question: *Do the needs of the many outweigh the needs of the one?* And just as often, the series asks the reverse: *When do the needs of the one override the needs of the many?* These are not mathematical problems. They are ethical judgments that require human empathy, real life context, and accountability to living things.

When we learn how to manage our ancient need to feel safe and survive in the modern world, we will not just grow stronger personally, we will gain a more effective and advanced "survival intelligence." We will rely less on our sympathetic nervous system for survival and more on our moral and thoughtful sympathetic feelings for others.

Resilience, or as I like to think of if it, Adaptive Intelligence, is *the* survival skill. And it's one we can teach, starting in childhood, so kids learn to recognize fear when it arises and how to transform that energy into constructive life-affirming actions.

This is a human evolution trajectory we can choose.

The End of the Lie

At the same time, humanity itself is changing in visible ways. As people move, intermingle, fall in love, and build families across the planet, we are becoming more alike in our physical traits by blending skin tones, facial features, and hair textures, as well as normalizing our cultural differences.

Maybe this will finally help put to rest the lies about race we've been told for generations. Those false stories were created to organize power, control resources, and justify domination. In biological terms, there is no such thing as multiple human races. *Homo sapiens* is a single species. We are one race: the human race.

And yet, many still live as if they are huddled in small tribes that must defend themselves from an imagined "other." That instinct once helped our ancestors survive. Today, it acts like an evolutionary blindfold, keeping us from seeing our shared fate on this planet.

Diversity Strengthens Us

Diversity brings opportunities for new evolutionary pathways. Our species has adapted and evolved because of variations in our genetics. It's how we survived disease, scarcity, and uncertainty across time. Every new variation is an opportunity for resilience. Traits once seen as problems can turn out to be protective.

I know someone whose immune system is permanently dialed up. While it requires medication to manage, that same trait could become a powerful adaptation for a future pandemic. Empaths who were once seen as "too sensitive" are teaching us how to use empathy to strengthen social bonds and increase collaboration. Neurodivergent individuals see patterns that others miss and are calling us to see the world from their unique perspectives.

We can also have diversity in behaviors. Some people today are reviving ancient behaviors, developing skills that rely upon a different kind of knowledge than traditional scientific reasoning. They pay attention to gut feelings or attempt to communicate or even travel telepathically across the ether.

While these traits are difficult to prove or measure, there

is an interesting trend that seems to be emerging. Humans are beginning to act in a more collective and connected way, as if we have a hive mind. When people follow a podcast to try to work together to solve a true-crime mystery, or when we try that viral recipe, or laugh at the shared meme for the day, we are connecting thoughts and attitudes at a rate we've never done before. When we send money, prayers, and care to those caught in a tragedy or disaster, we're exhibiting the best of our human potential.

As we explored in the chapter on quantum manifestation and "inter-being," we are not separate from one another. Our nervous systems, our thoughts, and our futures are intertwined through the potentialities. We rise and fall together.

The question is whether we will finally live like that's true?

The Future Belongs to the Emotionally Grounded

In the future, the most successful people won't just be the smartest. They'll be the most grounded and the most stable. I'm talking about you: someone who (maybe after reading this book) is more equipped to get themselves into a balanced "feel-good state." The people making decisions in homes, classrooms, hospitals, courtrooms, boardrooms, and space stations will be those who can stay grounded under pressure and act from values instead of fear.

Whether you're a server carrying a stack of pancakes at a diner or an AI CEO making a decision about whether to open a data center, your emotional state matters. We've learned that operating from fear narrows our world and feels awful to experience in both mind and body. How we seek relief from that feeling is what makes or breaks us.

The mask is already slipping from the old evolutionary relics of bullying, greed, domination, and punching down. We are beginning to see what lies behind those destructive fear-based behaviors. Making a single race "superior," putting the needs of one geographic area over another, dehumanizing "others," and trying to out-ego or out-greed your neighbor is not strength. It's insecurity, it's fear, and it's sad. Living like that does not feel good, at least not long-term.

When humans feel safe, connected, and regulated, we stop wasting energy on constant threat responses. We become more creative, and we rely upon the intelligence of our imagination (as Einstein demonstrated). We see the ethical response more easily and get better at problem-solving. When we learn to feel safe in a world of uncertainty, that's when our brains and bodies heal from trauma, and that's how we stop repeating the same destructive patterns generation after generation.

Feeling good isn't self-indulgent. It's the capacity to heal, to choose wisely, and to operate from calm rather than constant freak-out. We simply cannot live like ancient cave people for much longer. It's time for the heroes of today to step forward and call for a new way of living.

It's what I wanted for those rock-throwing boys back in

2006. And it's what I want for you.

14

RESOURCES

About These Resources:

The organizations listed on these pages are shared as options, not endorsements. Everyone's situation is different, and what feels helpful for one person may not feel right for another. We encourage you to try what feels safest, stop if something doesn't feel supportive, and explore other resources if needed.

Neither I nor my nonprofit, Bounce Back Generation, control or operate these services.

Please also visit Bounce Back Generation's website, bbgtv.org, for more information about the topics we talk about in the book, including the **6 Building Blocks**. We also have a YouTube Channel @bouncebackgeneration. In addition, this book is being offered as a free podcast on all podcast platforms and YouTube called: *How to Bounce Back: Emotional*

Evolution and the Science of Feeling Good.

You may also enjoy *How to Get Calm Before You Lose Your Cool: A Nervous System Guide for Parents, Educators, and Kids* by Jennifer Dhillon.

Resources current as of February 2026.

CRISIS SUPPORT (U.S. 24/7)

988 Suicide & Crisis Lifeline

Call or Text: 988

Chat available online. For emotional distress, suicidal thoughts, panic, or when things feel unbearable.

CRISIS TEXT LINE

Text HOME to 741741. Free, confidential texting with a trained crisis counselor.

SAMHSA National Helpline

1-800-662-HELP (4357). Mental health and substance-use support, treatment referrals, and information.

LGBTQIA+ SUPPORT

The Trevor Project

Call: 1-866-488-7386

Text: **988** (select LGBTQ+ option)

TRANS LIFELINE

Peer support run by and for trans people.

U.S.: 1-877-565-8860

Canada: 1-877-330-6366

LGBT National Help Center — Youth Talkline

1-800-246-7743. Peer support (set hours).

AFRICAN AMERICAN, BIPOC AND LGBTQ+ YOUTH

Call BlackLine

1-800-604-5841. Peer support prioritizing BIPOC communities, including LGBTQ+ youth.

FOSTER YOUTH, FORMER FOSTER YOUTH & SYSTEMS-INVOLVED YOUTH

Search online for the following:

FosterClub

Youth-friendly information on foster care, rights, education, housing, and transitions to adulthood.

Child Welfare Information Gateway

Trusted federal resource with guides for youth, caregivers, and advocates.

Youth Law Center (YLC)

Legal rights, advocacy tools, and explainers for foster and justice-involved youth.

CDSS Foster Youth Wellness Project — "Need Help Now"

Your Life Your Voice 1-800-448-3000 (preteens, teens, and young adults) Text "voice" to 20121

Crisis Text Line (anywhere in the USA) Text "youth" to 741741 to reach a trained counselor.

If you're outside California, FosterClub at https://www.fosterclub.com/

ABUSE, VIOLENCE, EXPLOITATION & UNSAFE SITUATIONS

Childhelp National Child Abuse Hotline

Call or Text: 1-800-422-4453

RAINN — Sexual Assault Hotline

1-800-656-HOPE (4673)

Online chat and text available.

National Domestic Violence Hotline

24/7 confidential support for unsafe relationships.

1-800-799-7233

Text: 88788

Love Is Respect

Call: 1-866-331-9474

Text: LOVEIS to 22522. Support for dating abuse and unhealthy relationships.

National Human Trafficking Hotline

Call: 1-888-373-7888

Text: 233733

Runaway, Homeless, or "I Can't Go Home"

National Runaway Safeline

1-800-RUNAWAY (786-2929)

Chat and text options available via their website:1800runaway.org/

211 (United Way)

Call: 211. Connects you to free local help: housing, food, counseling, healthcare, school support, and more.

FREE OR LOW COST PHYSICAL AND MENTAL HEALTH CARE

Search online for the following:

HRSA Health Centers

Community clinics with free or sliding-scale medical and mental health care.

National Institute of Mental Health (NIMH)

Science-based information on youth mental health and how to get help.

SCHOOLWORK, LEARNING & ACADEMIC SUPPORT

Khan Academy

Free tutoring and lessons (K-college).

211

Call or text: 211. Talk to a real person for local help.

Can help find local homework help, libraries, after-school programs, and tutoring.

Career and Personality Tests (Free)

Search for: The Foundation for Talent Transformation

"I DON'T KNOW WHAT I NEED. JUST HELP ME FIND IT"

If you're unsure where to start, these are excellent first stops. Search online for:

FindHelp.org — Search free services by ZIP code

NIMH Youth Mental Health Hub

Learn what's normal, what's not, and what to do.

International Crisis Support (Free)

https://www.helpguide.org/find-help

Canada: 988 (call or text)

United Kingdom & Ireland: Samaritans 116 123

UK (Under 19): Childline 0800 1111

Australia: Kids Helpline 1800 55 1800

TAKE THE ACE TEST

Adverse Childhood Experiences test with information can be found at https://developingchild.harvard.edu/resources/handouts-tools/take-the-aces-quiz/

Remember, a high ACEs score does not mean you will suffer all or even some of the developmental, emotional, or physical health effects. It can give you insight and information about the potential for these risk factors.

IMPORTANT TIPS AND THINGS TO KNOW

You do not have to be suicidal to use crisis lines. Feeling overwhelmed is enough. You can just call to talk.

Most services are confidential, but if someone believes your life is in immediate danger, emergency services *may* be contacted.

You can hang up, text STOP, or leave a chat at any time.

It's OK to try more than one resource until you find one that feels right.

BOOKS REFERENCED

Determined by Robert Sapolsky

The Body Keeps the Score by Bessel Van der Kolk

Sapiens by Yuval Noah Harari

Helgoland by Carlo Rovelli

Interbeing by Thích Nhất Hạnh

Dopamine Nation by Anna Lempke

These books are referenced for educational context and do not imply endorsement of all views expressed.

These resources are provided for informational purposes and are not a substitute for professional medical, legal, or mental health care.

About the author

Jennifer Dhillon is a resilience expert, attorney, and nonprofit leader with over 20 years of experience studying how humans adapt, survive, and grow through adversity. She is the founder of Bounce Back Generation, a nonprofit launched in 2011, and holds a degree in Development Studies from UC Berkeley. Her work draws on neuroscience, trauma studies, psychology, and lived experience supporting youth and families in crisis, including her current practice as a juvenile dependency and family law attorney.

She is also the author of *How to Get Calm Before You Lose Your Cool: A Nervous System Guide for Parents, Educators, and Kids*. Much of what she has learned comes from the resilient individuals and communities she has worked alongside.

Jennifer lives in California with her son, two dogs, and two cats.

About Bounce Back Generation

Bounce Back Generation is a youth-powered nonprofit helping young people build emotional strength, confidence, and calm in a world that feels like, and is, *a lot*. Through science-backed tools, storytelling, and real conversations about stress, trauma, and growth, we help kids and young adults learn how to regulate their nervous systems, understand their emotions, and see themselves as capable heroes in their own lives.

If you've ever thought, "*Why didn't anyone teach us this stuff sooner?*" That's exactly why we exist.

Your purchase of this and our other media offerings through Generation Bounce Back Media, helps us create free content, workshops, and resources for youth who need these tools the most. Visit our website at bouncebackgeneration.org, or bbgtv.org to learn more.

www.ingramcontent.com/pod-product-compliance
Lightning Source LLC
LaVergne TN
LVHW090316210926
848480LV00001B/271